School Activities and The Law

John L. Strope, Jr.

The National Association of Secondary School Principals
1904 Association Drive, Reston, Va. 22091

Executive Director: Scott D. Thomson
Director of Publications and Editorial Services: Thomas F. Koerner
Project Editor: Patricia Lucas George
ISBN 0-88210-158-7

About the Author

John L. Strope, Jr. is associate professor and chairman of the department of educational leadership and foundations at the University of South Alabama, Mobile. He completed his Doctor of Philosophy in educational administration and his Juris Doctor at the University of Nebraska.

In addition to teaching undergraduate and graduate courses on law, finance, personnel, and the principalship, Strope has written and lectured on these topics to numerous local, state, and national education groups.

Parts of this monograph are drawn from material originally prepared for Student Activities in the Secondary Schools, *a book published by Greenwood Press. It is reprinted by permission of the publishers.*

Contents

Foreword

Many of the legal questions that plagued educational administrators in the 1960s and '70s have been resolved, either by the courts or by educational authorities. Most of these questions involved student rights to attend school and receive an education, and, therefore, were cases that arose out of suspension or expulsion of students from school—usually as the result of school disciplinary infractions. Rarely, however, did courts address questions about student participation in cocurricular activities.

Since many of the issues centered on school attendance have been resolved in the 1980s, the courts and school boards are witnessing more questions about the extent of a school's authority to regulate student participation in cocurricular activities, which have grown in number and importance in the educational program. While a few authors have addressed the specific legal issues presented by school sports and athletic activities, to our knowledge, this monograph is the first to take up the broader legal concerns involved in student activities as a whole.

These legal issues are broader, of course, than those affecting school authority over student participation in such activities, and Strope addresses these too. The authority and liability of interscholastic associations at local, state, and regional levels has become one focus of considerable litigation. Liability of activity advisers, while not a new issue, is certainly one of continuing concern to all advisers, and we are hopeful that Strope's discussion, together with the National Association of Student Activity Advisers liability insurance program, will provide needed confidence and security to advisers.

Finally, some of the most perplexing issues of educational employment continue to arise out of the cocurricular assignments of activity advisers, and Strope has provided a good background to these legal issues. We hope advisers and administrators alike will profit from this material and avoid many of the pitfalls which have led to litigation in recent years.

As NASSP has often advised its members in the past, no monograph or book of any kind can take the place of appropriate legal advice, and the adviser or principal who expects it to would be unwise. But, many legal pitfalls can be avoided in advance by those involved in student activities if they are informed about legal issues. That is the purpose of this monograph. We believe that those administrators and advisers who keep it close at hand will find it of great value in keeping them out of trouble, while allowing them to carry out their work with greater confidence and proficiency.

Ivan Gluckman
Director, Legal Services
and Government Relations
NASSP

Chapter I

Introduction to The Law

"What is the law?"

Many people see the law as statutes passed by a legislative body such as a state legislature or the United States Congress. Others suggest more cynically that the law is what judges say it is in their opinions.

The law is much more, however. Law is not only legislative enactments, it is constitutions, court opinions, governing board policies, agency regulations, and coaches' rules.

United States Supreme Court decisions have said that a public school educator cannot afford *not* to know the law. Starting with the 1975 case of *Wood v. Strickland,* the Court has consistently held that violating a student's or teacher's federal rights can cause the educator to be liable for monetary damages and attorney fees to that individual.[1]

Even if an educator acts in ignorance of the law, depriving a student or teacher of federal constitutional and statutory rights such as freedom of speech, freedom of religion, due process of law, access to Chapter I, and freedom from discrimination can cost the institution and the individual money.

While imposing a penalty for malicious deprivation of federal rights is understandable enough, the Court added the element of deprivation of "basic," "settled," and "unquestioned" constitutional and statutory rights to expand a public school official's liability. Thus, a pure heart and an empty head can cost a principal money.

Educators need not be constitutional law scholars, but the Supreme Court has very definitely indicated that ignorance of the law is not an excuse. Educators must be familiar with settled, indisputable, and unquestioned federal rights. Such rights include: the ban on Bible reading or prayers in the public schools; segregation by race in classes; suspension or expulsion from school without due process of law; a rule requiring all students to salute the flag; and different grading policies for blacks or whites, or for males or females.

Thus, public school educators cannot sit back and use ignorance about the law as an excuse for violating someone's rights. An *affirmative obligation* now exists, backed by the threat of a monetary penalty, for educators to learn about the law.

A second area of potential monetary liability of all educators and for all educational institutions is tort liability—liability for injuries to persons or property. While educators have always faced the possibility of tort suits, in today's litigation-conscious society, such suits are especially prevalent.

This problem is compounded for the principal because student activities typically are characterized by non-classroom, physical activities. Hence, an appreciation of legal reasoning as it relates to tort liability may also save the educator from court-mandated damages for personal injuries.

Simply speaking, a legal system exists to resolve disagreements and to ensure that rules of fair play are followed. Where more than in the public and nonpublic schools is it important to teach that people must resolve their differences in a fair way? Therefore, an appreciation of law should encourage educators to function *more fairly* as well as more legally.

Sources of Relevant Law

If it is true that "law is all around us," then this is especially accurate when considering law, public schools, and student activities. Several sources of law relevant to schools can be identified. These include:

- United States Constitution
- Federal laws
- Federal agency regulations
- State constitutions
- State laws
- State board of education policies
- State department of education regulations
- Athletic/Activity association rules
- Local board of education policies
- Local administrative regulations
- Local school rules
- Coach/Sponsor rules
- Contracts with unions, teachers, parents, and students.

Two other significant sources should be added to this list—federal and state court decisions. In their efforts to resolve disputes and interpret laws, policies, and rules, courts necessarily "make" law. From all these sources come legal dictates that affect the operation of public school activity programs.

How does this discussion of school activities relate to nonpublic schools and their employees? Realistically, much of the law discussed here does not have relevance to nonpublic schools. Generally speaking, any discussion of federal constitutional and statutory rights only applies to *public* institutions and employees. Some exceptions relating to enrollment and employment discrimination exist.[2] Neither of these subjects is significantly treated in this publication.

Whether the material about athletic and activity association rules affects nonpublic schools depends on whether a school belongs to the association in its state. If the nonpublic school is a member, then the discussion is relevant. One area that most certainly applies to nonpublic schools is tort liability. As previously indicated, the law generally does not treat public schools and private schools differently with regard to liability for injuries suffered by students and employees, unless some degree of governmental immunity has been conferred upon the public schools by the state legislature.

Also, nonpublic schools may face legal problems in the treatment of students and teachers, not because of federal constitutional commands but because of contractual provisions made with these individuals.[3] Provisions in employment contracts, school handbooks, and bulletins, have a similar impact, as does a statute or constitutional provision in the public sector. Contract violations can also result in the awarding of monetary damages as a remedy for the injured party.

As the previous list illustrates, a hierarchy of laws exists in America. The United States Constitution is the supreme law of the land and no federal or state laws, policies, regulations, and rules can conflict with it. What's more, no state or local laws, policies, rules, or constitutions can conflict with federal laws or federal agency regulations. The list also identifies all sources of law that administrators must consider with relation to student activities. Finally, local school rules as well as coach or sponsor rules have the weight of law in the eyes of the legal system.

Judicial Attitudes Toward Control of Participants and Activities

Educators have supported student activities as part of a total school offering for many years, and for more than 50 years, courts have agreed with educators' support. In 1932, the Utah Supreme Court said:

> It is the aim of modern educators to expand the educational system so as to keep the interest and employ the energy of school children during their leisure time, and in this way prevent children from getting into mischief and becoming law violators. These are useful and wholesome preventive measures which save children from delinquency and the state from additional expense in connection with penal institutions.[4]

Though reasons for supporting student activities may have changed over the years, courts around the country have supported student activities' place in the school setting. Today's courts have said that these activities are "an integral and complimentary part of the total school program."[5]

Who should control these activities and how extensive should that control be? The Supreme Court has said:

> By and large public education in our nation is committed to control of state and local authorities. Courts do not and cannot intervene in the resolution of conflicts which arise in the daily operation of school systems. . . .[6]

Courts have extended this general rule to apply in the area of student activities.[7] Both federal and state courts have reiterated their belief that judgments about activities and participants in activities should be left to the discretion of local school officials. This view has been similarly expressed with regard to the decisions of state athletic and activity associations.[8] This discretion has been held to even supersede the wishes of parents.[9]

How far can control over participants and activities be extended?

In 1906, an Iowa school board adopted a policy disfavoring football because of potential injuries to students. To enforce its policy, the board suspended a student from school for playing in a weekend football game at a local fairgrounds. The game was advertised as a game between teams representing the school attended by the plaintiff and a neighboring school. Though the student's school had no official connection with the team or the game, the Iowa Supreme Court upheld this suspension as within the board's discretion where outside behavior affects the operation of the school.[10]

Although this ruling may not hold up today, the message is still strong. If an activity is related to the welfare of the school, when or where the activity is held will not likely diminish the authority of principals over student participants.

More recently, a senior high school student was suspended from cocurricular activities for three days and not allowed to participate in the senior class trip because upon seeing one of his teachers at a local shopping center, the student made a loud, derogatory remark about him. Though there was no express rule prohibiting such behavior, the federal court readily supported the principal's decision to punish the student for behavior detrimental to the school.[11]

Despite the breadth of their discretion, school officials do not have free reign over students. In the same breath that the Supreme Court recognized the dominant role of school officials in operating public schools, it reiterated a willingness to intervene judicially where constitutional freedoms are involved. In the landmark black armband case, *Tinker v. Des Moines Independent Community School District,* the Supreme Court found that neither students nor teachers shed their constitutional rights at the schoolhouse gate.[12]

In the wake of the *Tinker* decision, courts, especially federal courts, have been inundated with challenges to policies and decisions of school officials. Courts are torn between having to resolve these disputes either "against" the board or "against" the rights of students.

This dilemma of students' rights versus educators' authority often led courts to expound philosophically. A Texas judge wrote:

> Freedom after all is not something turned foot-loose to run as it will, like a thoroughbred in a bluegrass meadow. Freedom in a democracy is a matter of character and tolerance. The ideal recipient of it is one who voluntarily refuses to sacrifice the common good to personal passion.[13]

The Court of Appeals for the Fifth Circuit observed:

> *Tinker's* dam to school board absolutism does not leave dry the field of school discipline . . . *Tinker* simply irrigates rather than floods the fields of school discipline. It sets canals and channels through which school discipline might flow with the least possible damage to the nation's priceless topsoil of the First Amendment. Perhaps it would be well if those entrusted to administer the teaching of American History and Government to our students begin their efforts by practicing the documents on which that history and government are based.[14]

Perhaps Federal District Judge Pettine best explained this dilemma when he commented:

> This court's role, of course, is to not mandate social norms or impose its own view of acceptable behavior. It is instead, to interpret and apply the Constitution as best it can. The Constitution is not self-explanatory, and answers to knotty problems are inevitably inexact. All that an individual judge can do is to apply the legal precedents as accurately and honestly as he can, uninfluenced by personal predilections or the fear of community reaction, hoping each time to disprove the legal maxim that 'hard cases make bad law.'[15]

Studying a series of court opinions on a single subject is often interesting, demonstrating the dilemma judges face when trying to arrive at a balance between recognizing the vast discretion of school officials and protecting rights of students or teachers. The controversy over hair and grooming rules is an excellent example of the confusion that can abound.

In the late 1960s, many schools either adopted or began to enforce hair and grooming regulations—not only toward students in general, but especially toward students involved in athletics, student government, and other student activities. For every decision that can be found rejecting such rules, a decision just as convincing can be found supporting them.[16]

One of the most recent cases challenging the hair length rule included a study of court decisions around the country.[17] Research indicated that courts of appeals in the First, Third, Fourth, Seventh, and Eighth Circuits recognize a federal constitutional right in one's personal appearance, while the Fifth, Sixth, Ninth, and Tenth Circuits do not.

Fortunately, few cases have come before the courts since the mid-1970s. Perhaps the best commentary on the grooming cases came from Federal Judge Young, who sarcastically observed that school authorities and the complaining students' parents appeared "to be functioning at about the same level of maturity."[18]

However, another series of cases challenging the extent of board discretion led to a unanimous result. Over the years, school systems and athletic and activity associations enacted rules limiting or forbidding participation of married students in student activities. These prohibitions extended from athletics, to school offices, to attendance at social events like the junior-senior prom, senior breakfast, or awards night. Interestingly, these policies were considered an advancement from the previous situation in which school attendance as well as participation in cocurricular activities were forbidden to a married student.

Court decisions through the mid-1960s upheld such policies;[19] however, since then, courts have unanimously struck them down.[20] Courts have generally determined that these policies infringe upon the federal constitutional right to marry, and states and school districts are unable to demonstrate a compelling reason for such policies.

One further dimension of control over participants and activities requires discussion. Who has not heard a fellow educator lament that the courts are running the schools? Who has not heard the coach complain that he or she cannot discipline an athlete or that he or she will get sued, or that so much red tape is involved with due process that it is not worth it? Exactly what does "due process of law" mean? How does it apply to school activities?

The Supreme Court has indicated that any discussion of due process of law requires a two-part analysis.[21] The first step is to determine whether any federal constitutional liberty or property right is involved in the controversy. The second step, which comes *only* if the first part of the analysis is answered affirmatively, involves the nature of the process due to the complaining party.

The Fourteenth Amendment commands that no state "deprive a person of life, liberty, or property without due process of law." Over the years the federal courts have had to identify rights that fit the definition of life, liberty, and property. Within the school realm, the Supreme Court has identified the state-created right to attend school as a property right within the meaning of the Fourteenth Amendment.[22] Since that decision in 1975, numerous cases have come before state and federal courts in an effort to further define and expand that concept.

If one cannot be expelled or suspended from school without some due process, may one be excluded from a *portion* of the educational program without due process? For example: Can an athlete be suspended from a team without any notice of the charges or opportunity to present his or her side of the story at a formal or informal hearing? Almost unanimously courts have said that only *total* exclusion from the educational process requires any sort of notice and hearing, i.e., due process of law.[23] Thus, a student dropped from an athletic team or a student prohibited from participating in the senior class trip is not afforded, as a matter of federal law, any right to due process.[24]

There have been exceptions to the nearly unanimous general rule indicating that school officials can, without due process, exclude students from cocurricular activities. Certainty of one's legal position requires knowledge of relevant state law as well as knowledge of judicial decisions in that jurisdiction.

For example, within the jurisdiction of the Court of Appeals for the Eighth Circuit, the last 10 years have seen the development of the view that participation in cocurricular activities is a "significant" right.[25] That concept, somewhat erroneously taken out of context from a 1973 Eighth Circuit decision, has led both state and federal courts in the upper mid-western United States to treat participation in cocurricular activities as a protected property right within the meaning of the Fourteenth Amendment.[26]

In Pennsylvania, a federal court determined that a system's policies created a property interest in participating in interscholastic athletics.[27] Similarly, a federal district court in North Carolina ruled that total exclusion from participation in all cocurricular activities for a lengthy period of time could implicate a protected property right and thus require due process prior to the exclusion.[28] The New Hampshire Supreme Court held these activities to be "an integral and important element of the educational process."[29] These cases, however, are definitely the exception rather than the rule.

Plaintiffs in other cases involving exclusion from participation in activities have tried to identify losses as implicating property rights. Student athletes have claimed that exclusion from participating on a team would lead to a loss of future scholarship opportunities.[30] Courts have not generally accepted such arguments from secondary school students because the potential for actually securing any scholarship was too tenuous. Other circumstances could intervene which could also account for one's not receiving a scholarship.

If the court were to determine that no federal constitutional right to property were involved, would any kind of procedural procedure (due process) be due? No. One only has a constitutional right to due process when there is interference with some constitutionally protected right. Hence, across the country, no protected right generally exists, so no due process is required for removal from activities. However, in those jurisdictions where such participation is protected, the nature of the due process required must then be considered. Even while finding the existence of a protected right, courts have ruled that only the most minimal due process must then be given to the student.

The basic idea of due process of law involves notice of the charges and an opportunity for a hearing. With these cases, the courts have generally found that the principal or coach must only tell the student what the punishment is and why, and allow the student to explain his or her side of the story, before the decision takes effect. No formal hearing, no written notice of charges, no witnesses or cross-examination, and no legal counsel are required. Only the most minimal opportunity for a hearing after notice of the charges need be given.

Throughout this discussion of official authority and due process of law flows a general belief that decisions ought to be fair. Toward this end, fair procedure must be established and applied in a fair manner to participants in student activities.[31] The Supreme Court once stated that it had imposed standards no higher than a fairminded principal would impose upon himself.[32] In exercising the vast discretion to control student activities and participants, school board members, administrators, coaches, and sponsors are advised to create procedures that encourage arrival at a fair conclusion in fact.

Where state law, school board policies, or school rules have created such procedures and applied them fairly, courts usually have rejected plaintiff's arguments until they have given the process an opportunity to operate. While courts are not reluctant to become immediately involved when fundamental constitutional rights or tax funds are obviously involved, they are much less willing to enter typical disputes between students, teachers, and schools over school activity issues until all administrative remedies have been exhausted.[33]

Summary

Educators must see the "law" as being broader than state statutes. The Supreme Court has placed an obligation upon public school officials to know the rights of students and employees.

The other side of the legal coin is an overwhelming judicial propensity to support the rules and decisions of professional educators. Especially in the area of cocurricular activities, educators have been given a vast discretion to implement sound educational philosophies.

Footnotes

1. 420 U.S. 308 (1975); Harlow v. Fitzgerald, 73 L.Ed.2d 396 (1982).
2. Green v. Regan, ______ F. Supp. ______ (D. D.C. 1983).
3. Spell v. Bible Baptist Church, 303 S.E.2d 156 (Ga.App. 1983).
4. Beard v. Board of Educ., 16 P.2d 900 (Utah 1932).
5. Davis v. Meek, 344 F. Supp. 298 (N.D. Ohio 1972); Cape v. Tennessee Sec. Sch. Ath. Ass'n., 424 F. Supp. 732 (E.D. Tenn. 1976); Dunham v. Pulsifer, 312 F. Supp. 411 (D. Vt. 1970).
6. Epperson v. Arkansas, 393 U.S. 97 (1968).
7. Wood v. Strickland, 420 U.S. 308 (1975); Zeller v. Donegal Sch. Dist., 517 F.2d 600 (3rd Cir. 1975); Kernstein v. Pewaukee Sch. Bd., 557 F. Supp. 565 (E.D. Wis. 1983).
8. Oklahoma High Sch. Ath. Ass'n. v. Bray, 321 F.2d 269 (10th Cir. 1963).
9. Cordova v. Chonko, 315 F. Supp. 953 (N.D. Ohio 1970).
10. Kinzer v. Directors of Indep. Sch. Dist., 105 N.W. 686 (Iowa 1906).
11. Fenton v. Stear, 423 F. Supp. 767 (W.D. Pa. 1976).
12. 393 U.S. 503 (1969).
13. Passel v. Fort Worth Indep. Sch. Dist., 453 S.W.2d 888, 892 (Tex. Civ. App. 1970).
14. Shanley v. Northeast Indep. Sch. Dist., 462 F.2d 960, 978 (5th Cir. 1972).
15. Fricke v. Lynch, 491 F. Supp. 381, 389 (D. R.I. 1980).
16. *Cases decided for students:* Long v. Zopp, 476 F.2d 180 (4th Cir. 1973); Dostert v. Berthold Pub. Sch. Dist. #54, 391 F. Supp. 876 (D. N.Dak. 1975); Jacobs v. Benedict, 301 N.E.2d 723 (Ohio C.P. 1973); Cordova v. Chonko, 315 F. Supp. 953 (N.D. Ohio 1970); Dunham v. Pulsifer, 312 F. Supp. 411 (D. Vt. 1970). *Cases decided against students:* Neuhaus v. Torrey, 310 F. Supp. 192 (N.D. Calif. 1970); Corley v. Daunhauer, 312 F. Supp. 811 (E.D. Ark. 1970); Zeller v. Donegal Sch. Dist., 517 F.2d 600 (3rd Cir. 1975).
17. Dostert v. Berthold Pub. Sch. Dist. #54, 391 F. Supp. 876 (D. N.Dak. 1975).
18. Cordova v. Chonko, 315 F. Supp. 953 (N.D. Ohio 1970).
19. Kissick v. Garland Indep. Sch. Dist., 330 S.W.2d 708 (Tex. Civ. App. 1959); State v. Stevenson, 189 N.E.2d 181 (Ohio C.P. 1962); Board of Directors v. Green, 147 N.W.2d 854 (Iowa 1967).
20. Wimmer v. School Dist., No. 76-L-81 (D. Nebr. May 3, 1976); Davis v. Meek, 344 F. Supp. 298 (N.D. Ohio 1972); Romans v. Crenshaw, 354 F. Supp. 868 (S.D. Tex. 1972); Moran v. School Dist., 350 F. Supp. 1180 (D. Mont. 1972); Holt v. Shelton, 341 F. Supp. 821 (M.D. Tenn. 1972); Indiana High Sch. Ath. Ass'n. v. Raike, 329 N.E.2d 66 (Ind. App. 1975).
21. *See, e.g,* Goss v. Lopez, 419 U.S. 565 (1975).
22. *Id.* at 573.
23. Albach v. Odle, 531 F.2d 983 (10th Cir. 1976); Hamilton v. Tennessee Sch. Ath. Ass'n., 552 F.2d 681 (6th Cir. 1976).
24. Fenton v. Stear, 423 F. Supp. 767 (W.D. Pa. 1976).
25. Brenden v. Independent Sch. Dist., 477 F.2d 1292 (8th Cir. 1973); Teare v. Board of Educ., No. 77-L-190 (D. Nebr. Sept. 16, 1977).
26. Braesch v. De Pasquale, 265 N.W. 2d 842 (Nebr. 1978); Compagno v. Nebraska Sch. Act. Ass'n., No. 77-L-192 (D. Nebr. Sept. 16, 1977); Teare v. Board of Educ., No. 77-L-190 (D. Nebr. Sept. 16, 1977).

27. Davis v. Central Dauphin Sch. Dist., 466 F. Supp. 1259 (M.D. Pa. 1979).
28. Pegram v. Nelson, 469 F. Supp. 1134 (M.D. N.C. 1979).
29. Duffley v. New Hampshire Interscholastic Ath. Ass'n., 446 A.2d 462, 467 (N.H. 1982).
30. Kentucky High Sch. Ath. Ass'n. v. Hopkins City Bd. of Educ., 552 S.W.2d 685 (Ky. App. 1977).
31. Clark County Bd. of Educ. v. Jones, 625 S.W.2d 586 (Ky. App. 1981).
32. Goss v. Lopez, 419 U.S. 565 (1975).
33. Braesch v. De Pasquale, 265 N.W.2d 842 (Nebr. 1978); Ector County Indep. Sch. Dist. v. Hopkins, 518 S.W.2d 576 (Tex. Civ. App. 1974).

Chapter II

Control of Students

Contrary to the popular belief held by many principals, the courts have left them with extensive control over students involved with cocurricular activities. Except where basic fundamental constitutional rights are involved, student challenges to administrative decisions are usually unsuccessful.

Athletics by the Rules

In the previous chapter, the extensive discretion of school boards was emphasized and its legal support explained. Athletic and activity associations enjoy similar freedom to control their own business. Courts have long recognized that voluntary associations should conduct their affairs as their members see fit without judicial interference.[1]

Sometimes, courts will intervene to review, if not reverse, the rules and decisions of private associations. As in the cases involving schools, legal challenges focus on three questions:

1. Is the challenged rule or decision within the legal authority of the association?
2. Is the challenged rule or decision a reasonable exercise of that authority?
3. Is the rule fairly applied under the circumstances?

One Iowa case, *Bunger v. Iowa High School Athletic Association,* illustrates the scope of these challenges.[2] The IHSAA had adopted a good conduct rule that prohibited beer drinking. The rule and its interpretation mandated six weeks of interscholastic athletic ineligibility for athletes charged with consumption or possession of alcoholic beverages or who were in a vehicle in which alcoholic beverages were contained.

One evening during summer vacation, William Bunger was a passenger in a car that was stopped by a highway patrolman. While the other three minors pleaded guilty to possession of beer, Bunger pleaded not guilty and the charges were eventually dropped. Following the required procedure, he reported the incident to his school athletic director, admitted he knew the beer was in the car, and was declared ineligible for the first six weeks of the fall football season.

Bunger claimed that the association did not have the legal authority to promulgate the beer rule. Specifically, he argued that Iowa constitutional provisions and statutes delegated control of public education to the legislature and local boards and that it could not be re-delegated to the athletic association.

The Iowa Supreme Court agreed. The court recognized that IHSAA rules were not rules of each individual school and thus made and interpreted by each school. However, Iowa law established a procedure whereby IHSAA rules could be promulgated under the rule-making authority of the state board of public instruction. While other IHSAA rules had followed the process for legal authenticity, the good conduct rule and the beer rule had not. Thus, the rule was invalid.

As a second argument, Bunger claimed that the rule was not a reasonable rule. The rule, he argued, affected behavior beyond the school's authority to control. Courts had long recognized that schools could control behavior that directly related to the welfare and good order of the school. The court recognized that the influence of athletes and leaders upon other students justified extending the authority of a school board. While finding no problem with imposing ineligibility for beer drinking during the season, the court also expressed probable approval of such a rule for unconvicted possession or use during summer vacation. However, a penalty for merely being in the presence of alcohol outside of football season, beyond the school year, and with no evidence of illegal or improper use, went too far. Again the court ruled for the plaintiff.

Though not raised specifically in the *Bunger* case, a third challenge could question whether a legally-adopted, reasonable rule was fairly applied to the individual plaintiff. Such a challenge could focus on claimed inequities in enforcement—blacks versus whites, males versus females, athletes versus non-athletes. The constitutional command that no state deprive a person of equal protection of the laws is often at issue.[3]

Other arguments could center upon the fairness of the penalty. How much is too much punishment for a given misbehavior? Also, plaintiffs may question the fairness of the process used to determine the guilt. A claimed denial of due process of law will be based on the provision of the Fourteenth Amendment to the United States Constitution which asserts that no state shall deprive a person of life, liberty, or property without due process of law.

Clarification of "state" and "property" is required. Is a school board "state" for purposes of the Fourteenth Amendment? Is an athletic association "state" for purposes of the Fourteenth Amendment? The first question is easily answered in the affirmative. As a creature of the state, local school boards are included in the meaning of state. As to athletic associations, courts have debated the issue for years. Today the actions of athletic associations are unanimously characterized as state actions for legal purposes.[4]

Having given broader meaning to state, the discussion of due process focuses on the existence of a threat to life, liberty, or property. The discussion centers on whether participation in cocurricular activities is a property right. Almost unanimously the courts have said it is *not:* therefore, no notice and hearing are required before the penalty is imposed.[5] Later discussion in this chapter will highlight exceptions to this general rule.

General Transfer Rules

Most state athletic associations have a transfer rule that renders a student ineligible for participation for a stated period of time (semester or school year) upon transfer from one high school to another. These transfer rules are intended to prevent recruitment of student athletes. Associations mitigate the impact of the rule by not applying the penalty when the student moved because the parents have moved. Many states allow requests for hardship exceptions where the student is involuntarily denied the opportunity to remain living with the parents.

The courts have not been receptive to plaintiff challenges to transfer rules. One court after another has determined that the need to prevent recruiting outweighs the seemingly unfair effects of applying these rules with little or no consideration of actual motives behind the transfer. Most courts have found no property rights involved, so federal claims to due process of law are to no avail.[6] Challenges based on burdening the constitutional right to interstate travel have also been turned aside.[7] The ultimate support for these rules came from a Texas court which upheld a transfer rule barring competition in football or basketball for one year *even though* the parents themselves changed residence (from Vermont to Texas).[8] The rule was uniformly applied not only to interstate moves but to local intrastate moves as well. On appeal, however, the Supreme Court of Texas found the rule violated the Equal Protection Clause because the rule, and its application, were not reasonably related to the goal of deterring recruitment.

Plaintiffs often attempt to prove that the application of the rule, not the rule itself, is unfair in their particular circumstances. They have generally failed to find judicial support, although a Florida youngster who moved to Indiana to live in a more "wholesome environment" with his adult brother as legal guardian did win his case.[9]

Courts have tended to accept the associations' argument that a case-by-case decision would be a horrendous administrative burden.[10] Even in a state like Indiana where case-by-case determinations of transfer motives are apparently required, student athletes can still lose. One of the association's investigations uncovered a legal guardianship created for athletic purposes and evidence of undue influence. Hence, the transfer rule was applied.[11]

Transfers and Private Schools

Some of the most complicated transfer rules, and seemingly unfair applications of them, have involved ineligibility and attendance at private schools. Although freedom of religion seems burdened by these transfer rules, courts have unanimously supported the rules and their application.[12] When several cases in which the student athletes lost are reviewed, the extent of athletic association authority can be better recognized.

A Louisiana high school student could not return to his parochial high school because a school rule prohibited attendance by married students.[13] He discovered he would be ineligible for participation in athletics if he attended the local public school which served the attendance area in which his apartment was located, because his parents had not moved to that area. To maintain his eligibility, his parents moved in with the newlyweds. When the athletic association investigated, it determined that the move was not a bona fide change of residence, and the player remained ineligible to play *anywhere* during his senior year.

A slightly different application of the same Louisiana High School Athletic Association rule affected every student who attended the only Lutheran high school in the New Orleans metropolitan area.[14] The attendance districts of private schools were determined by the boundaries of the local public high school in which that private school was physically located. Because no Lutheran elementary or junior high schools were located within the boundaries of the district in which the Lutheran high school was located, all students who enrolled were treated as transfers under the rule and were ineligible for one year. Due to the indirect effect on religion and the lack of an equally effective and workable alternative, the rule as applied was upheld.

Finally, a Nebraska case demonstrates that the student has the burden to find out about the rule and be sure he or she is in compliance.[15] A job transfer led Vincent Compagno to move with his family from Denver to Omaha. In Nebraska, school districts are voluminous, and their boundaries are irregular and unrelated to city limits. Although the new residence was located one block inside of the Millard School District, which is a suburban district adjoining Omaha, it was still within the Omaha city limits. Since there was no Catholic school in the Millard district, Compagno enrolled at the nearest Catholic high school in Omaha which, he subsequently learned, was located in yet a third school district.

As with the typical transfer rule, Compagno was found not to be attending a school within the public school district where the family resided and could not attend a private school and be immediately eligible for interscholastic sports. Here, however, the student had no notice of the rule, and the court found the wording of the rule was probably not understandable to lay persons. Nevertheless, because the student made no effort to learn about potential eligibility questions and because it would have been virtually impossible for the association to have given Compagno notice of the rule before it was too late, the athlete lost.

Throughout these cases challenging transfer rules and their application, courts have found that the prevention of recruiting overrides almost any other consideration. Apparently, the best protection for students is for schools to work diligently to make eligibility rules known and their consequences appreciated.

Boys' Teams, Girls' Teams, and Coed Teams

In 1972, when Debbie Reed successfully brought suit in a federal court in Nebraska, her situation was typical of that faced by female athletes around the country.[16] Athletic opportunities for girls were severely limited or nonexistent. In Reed's case, no girls' golf team existed, although there was a boys' team. Girls also faced the constraints of school athletic association rules which forbade interscholastic competition by coed teams.

Reed and other cases of that era were built on a denial of equal protection of the laws guaranteed by the Fourteenth Amendment.[17] Plaintiffs argued that their inability to participate in interscholastic athletics was solely based on classification as female. Defendants, which included athletic associations and school boards, countered with the arguments that this was not a matter for the federal courts; males would dominate the teams; and girls would be subjected to a high risk of injury. Where non-contact sports were involved and, especially where no separate but equal team for girls existed, courts generally resolved these controversies in favor of the plaintiffs.

By the mid 1970s, cases were filed wherein females wanted to participate on boys' teams regardless of the existence of a separate girls' team. They argued that the caliber of competition on girls' teams was inferior to that on the boys' teams. Simultaneously, Title IX and its regulations appeared.[18] Pertinent provisions of that law and its regulations are designed to eliminate discrimination on the basis of sex in education programs and activities receiving federal financial assistance.

In particular, one regulation specifically addressed the issue of discrimination in athletic programs based upon sex. This regulation, in part, provides:

> . . . a recipient may operate or sponsor separate teams for members of each sex where selection for such teams is based upon competitive skill or the activity involved is a contact sport. However, where a recipient operates or sponsors a team in a particular sport for members of one sex but operates or sponsors no such team for members of the other sex, and athletic opportunities for members of that sex have previously been limited, members of the excluded sex must be allowed to try out for the team offered unless the sport

involved is a contact sport. For the purposes of this part, contact sports include boxing, wrestling, rugby, ice hockey, football, basketball and other sports the purpose or major activity of which involves bodily contact.[19]

In resolving these cases now, the courts consider both the impact of the equal protection clause of the Fourteenth Amendment as well as Title IX. While the law is anything but settled, especially in terms of the impact of Title IX, two cases provide some insight. A federal district judge in Michigan concluded that Title IX actually had no application in a controversy surrounding a female athlete who wanted to participate on the boys-only golf team.[20] His decision focused on the view that Title IX applied only to activities that receive direct federal money and, because no federal money went to athletics, Title IX could not be the basis for a claim in federal court.

It is probably too early to tell whether this Michigan case will represent the prevailing view of the law relating to Title IX, although its implications go well beyond interscholastic athletics.[21]

An Illinois sixth grade girl was prevented by athletic conference rules from participating on a boys' basketball team. Evidence indicated that equal funding and facilities were provided for the girls' team, but that she was capable and wanted to play on the boys' team so she would face better competition and develop her own athletic skills.

Was she denied equal protection of the laws? The Court of Appeals for the Seventh Circuit concluded no such deprivation had occurred because the state had a rational basis for the separate teams.[22] The state's objective was to maximize female participation in athletics. From the girl's point of view, her opportunities to participate were denied, but the court noted that seeming unfairness to one plaintiff must not itself cause the rule to be invalidated. Was the plaintiff denied any rights under Title IX? The court concluded that the previously-quoted regulation (§86.41b) expressly permitted two teams and exclusion of girls from contact sports. The United States Supreme Court refused to accept the case for review.[23]

Plaintiffs have another potential basis for a judicial claim. Individual states may have constitutional or statutory provisions which legislatively authorize or have been judicially interpreted to authorize rights of participation beyond those interpreted from the equal protection clause of the Constitution or Title IX.

These provisions led a Washington state court to invalidate a Washington Interscholastic Activities Association rule prohibiting females from participating on male teams in contact sports.[24] The court thereby allowed a girl to try out for the boys' football team.

Once the controversy over girls wanting to participate on boys' teams got enough attention, it inevitably followed that boys would argue for participation on previously all-girl teams like volleyball and softball. Such challenges have generally been unsuccessful because the courts have considered both the language and the spirit of Title IX and the equal protection clause to focus upon ensuring and increasing *female* athletic opportunities.[25] The conclusion was that boys would begin to dominate those sports because of their generally superior physical qualifications and take the place of aspiring female athletes.

The Massachusetts Supreme Judicial Court, based on particular provisions of the Massachusetts Equal Rights Amendment, invalidated an athletic association rule that prohibited boys from participating on girls' teams, but that case is probably the exception rather than the rule.[26]

The Minnesota Supreme Court looked philosophically at an athletic association rule which resulted in separate seasons and separate teams.[27] Schools presented evidence to demonstrate the inadequacy of facilities to serve both boys' and girls' tennis teams and swimming teams during the same seasons. A compromise established boys' and girls' seasons for these sports at different times during the year. Based on the practicalities of the situation, the court upheld the scheduling scheme, although it explicitly expressed its preference for teams which were not segregated on the basis of gender.

One other related question has come before the courts in recent years. Since the late 1970s, at least four states have operated girls' basketball programs under different rules than boys' basketball. In those four states, the so-called "half-court" game was played wherein three members play as forwards and neither group crosses the center line.

Plaintiffs argued that they were denied the full development of their skills, the full pleasure of the game, the opportunity for intensive physical conditioning, and the chances for college athletic scholarships. Defendants countered with the arguments that games were more exciting because they were higher scoring, more girls could participate, half-court games actually require more agility and skill, the half-court game is better adapted to the differing physical characteristics and capabilities of females, and the game had become a tradition in the state.

While the challenge in Arkansas succeeded, challenges in Oklahoma and Tennessee failed.[28] Again the equal protection clause and Title IX were bases for the plaintiffs' claims and, interestingly, all three courts interpreted their impact differently in arriving at their decisions.

Some unanswered questions still exist in this area. How "equivalent" is providing girls with volleyball and boys with football or girls with softball and boys with baseball? Can girls be deprived of the opportunity to participate in contact sports by the unilateral decision of the athletic association?

On this issue, the Court of Appeals for the Sixth Circuit indicated that such a decision must be based on the individual determinations of school systems that are recipients of federal financial assistance; individual boards may view the previous and current opportunities available to female athletes in their system differently.[29]

How different can the activities actually be and still be equal? This is a question similar to that raised in the boys' versus girls' basketball rules. In gymnastics, girls use uneven parallel bars. In swimming or track, the particular events may be shorter or conducted differently for females.

Given the tenor of the times, the best course of action is to provide athletic opportunities that are separate, but are as equal as possible and to allow mixed team competition when ability earns such a position. Judicial challenges to prohibitions based purely on participants' sex are not likely to disappear in the foreseeable future.

Participation of the Handicapped

One of the problems administrators of athletic programs faced during the 1970s involved participation of handicapped athletes. The number of reported cases on this subject is relatively small, so broad generalizations are both difficult and uncertain. Passage of the Rehabilitation Act of 1973, which included the provision popularly referred to as "Section 504" (§504), has not made resolution of these issues any simpler:

> No otherwise qualified handicapped individual in the United States, as defined in section 706(6) of this title, shall, solely by reason of his handicap, be excluded from participation in, be denied the benefits of, or be subjected to discrimination under any program or activity receiving Federal financial assistance.[30]

In two New York cases in the mid '70s, high school athletes with physical handicaps (eye and ear) challenged local school board decisions that were based on the recommendation of the board's medical officer that the dangers in contact sports were too great to permit participation.[31] In those cases, even where medical testimony conflicted, the decisions of the boards were judicially upheld. However, a 1978 New York state case was decided in favor of the plaintiff on essentially the same facts.[32]

Ironically, the victorious plaintiff had originally filed her complaint in a New York federal court claiming a violation of §504.[33] All cases brought under §504 require consideration of three questions:

1. Is the plaintiff a handicapped individual as defined in the law?
2. Does the activity or program receive federal financial assistance?
3. Is the plaintiff an otherwise qualified handicapped individual who is being excluded from participation solely by reason of the handicap?

In denying the plaintiff's request for a preliminary injunction, the federal court concluded that the plaintiff was not "otherwise qualified" because of the reasonableness of the determination that the risks in participation were too great.[34] The student went to state court and won on the basis of state law.

A recent New York case offers a similar analysis and conclusions with regard to §504,[35] although the complaint did not involve participation in an athletic program. The student had such serious, congenital physical handicaps that a full-time aide and special transportation and movement provisions were necessary during the regular school day. In considering the plaintiff's request to participate in a school-sponsored trip to Spain, the school board determined that the student would have to have an aide accompany her to deal with the physical handicaps.

When the family expressed an unwillingness to provide the aide, the board refused the student's request to participate. Apparently the federal court was indicating that while §504 might create demands for the regular school program, it did not necessarily place similar burdens on the school system for all school-related activities or for portions of a particular activity.

It is also important to recognize that the court easily dealt with the question of whether this was a program or activity receiving federal financial assistance. The court simply concluded that even though the students were paying a substantial portion of the cost of the trip, the school district that had planned and sponsored the program was a general recipient of federal financial aid, although none was directed explicitly toward this activity.

A controversy in Texas caused a federal court to determine that §504 must take precedence over the application of a typical athletic association transfer rule.[36] Because he was suffering severe psychiatric difficulties, the court concluded that the plaintiff was handicapped within the meaning of the statute. Living with his grandparents (even though his parents were living in another Texas community) and participating in interscholastic football represented a reasonable way to serve the needs of this handicapped child. To prevent his being discriminated against because of his handicap, the court granted a request for a preliminary injunction.[37] No trial was ever held.

However, the case became more significant because of a decision by the Court of Appeals for the Fifth Circuit following an appeal by the athletic association. The question of attorney fees faced the appellate court: did the federal statute permit awarding attorney fees in cases involving deprivation of civil rights in these §504 cases? The court concluded that attorney fees were possible and remanded the case to the district court for determination of the amount of attorney fees.[38]

Although the student had graduated, the athletic association was left with the specter of paying several thousand dollars in attorney fees for having originally refused to allow the student to participate. At that time, the Texas University Interscholastic League had no provisions to consider hardship exceptions to the general transfer rule; such process might have eliminated the loss of such a case in court.

Age/Attendance Requirements

Most athletic associations have rules prohibiting 19-year-olds from participation or limiting participation to four years or eight semesters of continuous attendance after the beginning of the ninth grade. Some states begin monitoring the continuity of grade level progression as early as sixth grade to ensure that any failures are for academic purposes only. These rules are intended to ensure fair competition, protect the younger and less mature athletes from older athletes, prevent academic decisions from being made for athletic purposes, and avoid rewarding academic failure.

Two Florida cases represent exceptions to the consistent course of judicial opinions that uphold these rules both as written and as applied.[39] In both instances, a Florida state appellate court determined that the hardship committees should have considered the students' evidence as sufficient grounds for granting an additional period of eligibility under the undue hardship exception. Such decisions stand in contrast to the generally-held view the plaintiff has to demonstrate the unreasonableness of the decision.

Even the special circumstances surrounding the students' request that these rules not apply have not changed the outcome. Two Missouri student-athletes had experienced extensive health problems during their younger years, causing them to be excluded from athletic competition during their senior years.[40] A Georgia student quit high school for a year and a half to help support his widowed mother who was suffering emotional illness. The rules were supported in both instances.[41]

Out-of-School Incidents

Greater meaning will be given to this analysis of cases if read in conjunction with the discussions surrounding the *Bunger* case and with the discussion at the beginning of the monograph about the extent of school board and athletic association authority. These cases concern ineligibility determinations because of incidents not directly related to the school setting or participation as a team member.

Athletic associations maintain rules which limit if not completely prohibit participation in a sport outside the school setting during the course of that particular interscholastic sport. Plaintiffs are not usually very successful in these cases. In other cases in which courts did not find property interests that are protected by due process of law, athletic associations demonstrate judicially-accepted rational bases for this rule by emphasizing the need to protect student health, avoiding interference with school work, maintaining a concern for the whole team, and protecting interscholastic competition from exploitation by those sponsoring the outside events. Once again, courts did not consider the fairness of the application of the rule upon individuals, but rather considered the rule in the abstract.

Whether the student had notice of the rule *prior* to imposition of ineligibility may be a factor. However, in only one case did the outcome turn on the question of notice.[42] Plaintiffs have lost when they had no notice of these rules as well as when they had notice.[43] In one case, the court did not even consider the question of whether the plaintiffs had notice of the rule.[44] In another, the court pointed out that the evidence conflicted about what high school coaches knew and said, about what Babe Ruth League coaches knew and said, and about what the student-athletes actually knew, and still the student lost his eligibility.[45]

One exception involved a New York high school girl who practiced with a college team after failing to make the boys' soccer team and after being told that it was too late to try out for the girls' team.[46] Originally, the no-outside-participation rule provided for loss of all future eligibility in any interscholastic sports, but, upon appeals following association procedures, the penalty was reduced to one year. The athletic association argued for the presumption that "all people know the law." The New York state court found that the association had offered no evidence that the plaintiff knew or should have known about the rule. This case, which held that the burden was on the association rather than the student to prove the student knew about the rule, is a gross exception to the common view of courts about the matter of notice of athletic association rules.

Athletes have also challenged rules which prohibited or limited outside athletic participation outside the season *and* outside the school year itself.[47]

Again, courts have found no federal constitutional rights, and the associations have demonstrated a rational basis for such rules. The associations have argued that the rule is intended to control over-zealous coaches and parents, protect student athletes from undue pressure, prevent the wealthy from enjoying special benefits, avoid the use of camps for recruiting purposes, prevent conflicts in approaches between school coaches and camp instructors, and assist student development by exposure to numerous sports at an early age.

A New Hampshire case demonstrates the creativity of the judicial mind which allowed the court to recognize the same principles of upholding these ineligibility rules while assuring a result for the plaintiff.[48] In the spring of 1971, after the conclusion of the high school basketball season, a student played in an Order of DeMolay-sponsored basketball tournament. The principal, according to testimony, wished the students good luck as they went off to the tournament. Soon after their return, the principal notified the plaintiff of his ineligibility to participate based on a New Hampshire Interscholastic Athletic Association rule that required ineligibility for one calendar year. This incident had occurred in the spring of the year, and the court determined that "calendar year" must mean January 1 to December 31 of the year in which the incident occurred. Therefore, the student would be ineligible until January 1, 1972. Seemingly, the student would miss little, if any, of the 1971-72 basketball season due to this imaginative interpretation of the rule.

Team and School Penalties

What have been the nature of the team and school penalties levied and for what reasons have the penalties been imposed? For using three academically ineligible players, one school was required to forfeit three football victories and thus be eliminated from state playoffs.[49] Another school was required to forfeit its league championship as well as the playoff receipts for having used a transfer player when the association determined that the parents' move was not a bona fide move within the meaning of the rule.[50]

Aliquippa High School in Pennsylvania was required to forfeit all football and basketball games during 1973 and 1975 in which academically ineligible players were used;[51] the school board, the high school principal, and the football and basketball coaches during those seasons were also officially censured; and the football and basketball teams were ineligible for playoff competition from 1976 through the 1978 school year.

For violation of an anti-recruiting rule, an Ohio high school was prohibited from fielding a football team for one year, and the two boys involved were declared forever ineligible to participate in interscholastic sports at that school.[52]

Fighting after a football game caused a Pennsylvania high school to be officially censured, placed on two-year probation, and prohibited from holding practice or athletic events after 4 p.m.[53]

The Louisiana High School Athletic Association promulgated a rule making individual schools responsible for the behavior of their supporters.

After a full hearing, the association found Fenton High School guilty of unsportsmanlike conduct because a spectator had abused a referee after a basketball game.[54] As a penalty, for a one-year period the school could not participate in events at which that spectator attended.

A Florida case illustrates the expansive authority given to the athletic associations by the courts.[55] When his parents divorced, Chris Bradshaw changed residence and became ineligible under a typical transfer rule. He suited up for two games although he never played. When the violation was discovered, an application was made for a hardship ruling, and the association granted the request. However, the association then required the high school to forfeit the two football games for having an ineligible player, despite the fact the violation was unknown, no recruiting was involved, and the association was willing subsequently to give the athlete a hardship exception! The association won.

The courts have consistently indicated an unwillingness to interfere with operations of private, voluntary associations. If the penalties or rules are too harsh, the courts tell the complaining parties to go back to the association and work to change the rules.

Again, outcomes do not differ just because many innocent individuals are penalized in the process of imposing the penalty. Even the arguments of the spectator in the Louisiana case—that she was being deprived of First Amendment rights of free speech, free association, freedom of assembly, privacy, and procedural due process—did not convince the court.[56] The Louisiana state court concluded that even if there were a constitutional right to participate in athletics or a constitutional right to attend athletic events, all participation is subject to reasonable non-discriminatory limitations, and crowd control represented a reasonable objective.

Another Louisiana case represents one example of a plaintiff's successful complaint about the application of a rule and subsequent penalty.[57] Early in the 1978 school year, a teacher-coach in a Catholic high school spoke to students at a Catholic elementary school about the scholastic and athletic programs at his school. After conducting an investigation, the association found the school and coach in violation of an undue influence rule and imposed certain penalties on the school.

The coach's claim of a denial of his freedom of speech under the First Amendment was dismissed by the trial judge without any trial. The coach claimed that the rule was vague as written and thus not reasonable or understandable. He also argued that his exercise of free speech was penalized by the association. On appeal, the Court of Appeals for the Fifth Circuit reversed the decision of the lower court and remanded the case for trial to allow the plaintiffs to prove their alleged constitutional violation.

It must also be remembered that a penalty unsupported by any credible evidence can be disallowed by a court. When a Texas association's imposition of penalties on certain boys' baseball and basketball teams was challenged in court, neither the trial nor the appellate judges could find *any* evidence to substantiate the charges.[58]

Regardless of the outcome of these two cases, the extensive authority of the athletic association to impose penalties for rules' violation remains undiminished.

Miscellaneous Cases

The cases discussed in this section are generally unrelated to each other, although the first cases do relate to freedom of religion.

Some conference and athletic association rules bar membership by private schools. Federal courts have upheld the rules in two recent judicial challenges.[59] No burden on the free exercise of religion was found while a rational basis for the exclusion was demonstrated. Because private schools generally have no defined attendance areas, enforcement of transfer and anti-recruitment rules would be impossible.

A membership requirement of the Arkansas Activities Association was challenged as a burden on the free exercise of religion by a denominational school. To join the association, a school was required to satisfy accreditation standards of the Arkansas State Department of Education. The church school rejected any elements of state authority over the operation of the school and had no intention of seeking state accreditation. The Court of Appeals for the Eighth Circuit upheld the association's rule.[60]

A ban on wearing yarmulkes (skullcaps) during basketball games was challenged by Orthodox Jewish student-athletes. Their religious beliefs, they alleged, required their heads be covered unless the students were unconscious, immersed in water, or in immediate danger of losing their lives. For some time these athletes had been allowed to wear the yarmulkes with no incidents of injury to any players.

Model rules of the National Federation of State High School Associations were adopted by the Illinois association, however, and included a ban on this apparel. Neither the National Federation nor the state association had any evidence of even one instance of injury caused by the wearing of yarmulkes. In fact, the National Federation had conducted a survey of coaches and found that they were overwhelmingly in favor (6 to 1) of retaining a previous rule which allowed the wearing of soft berets to which the yarmulkes were very similar. The court determined that a fundamental right to the free exercise of one's religion was burdened by this rule and prohibited its enforcement. However, the Court of Appeals remanded the case to explore the safety question and the specifics of the religious requirements further.[61]

Plaintiffs were successful with their judicial challenges in the following four cases:

- Illinois law provided a process for transferring real property from one school district to a neighboring school district for the educational welfare of the pupils involved.[62] The home system had no tennis team, and the athlete wanted to participate on such a team. The parents followed the process of transferring their property to a neighboring system which had a tennis team.
- A Florida Activities Association rule limited the number of players who could suit up for state football playoffs to 44 players after having allowed an unlimited roster during the season.[63] Both the trial court and appellate court found the rule to be arbitrary and irrational. The trial judge stated:

> Football is an American tradition which has formed a great cornerstone in shaping the lives of literally millions of Americans. It is uniquely adapted to educating our youth to the unquestioned merit of mental and physical discipline, wholesome and worthy competition under rules of good sportsmanship and fair play, and the achievement of excellence. Americans who have drawn upon their early lessons in football include Presidents Reagan, Kennedy, and Eisenhower and Supreme Court Justice White. Thus, while football may be a privilege, it is an essential part of the American educational mosaic.[64]

- A South Dakota school system sued the activities association because its policies discriminated against schools with small enrollment by allowing schools with the largest enrollments to have two chances to qualify for the national tournament of the National Forensic League. The federal court found an unlawful denial of the equal protection of the laws.[65]
- Many states recently adopted open meeting laws to assure that the public can monitor the activities of public officials. A television news director was denied access to a committee meeting of the Louisiana High School Association. He successfully argued that for purposes of the open meeting law the association was a public body and its meetings must be open to the public.[66]

The following cases, although factually unrelated to each other, have a common message—courts are generally staying out of the business of athletic associations:

- A South Dakota rule required that prior to participation in athletics, a health statement must be secured from a medical doctor or a licensed four-year-college-trained osteopath. A student wanted to secure his health statement from a chiropractor. The court upheld the rule.[67]
- A Georgia football referee had admittedly assessed an incorrect penalty and adversely affected the playoff hopes of a high school football team. In reversing the trial court, the Supreme Court of Georgia said that plaintiffs had no constitutional rights involved and that state courts in Georgia had no authority to review the decisions of football referees.[68]
- A runner claimed that a foul by a competitor kept him from qualifying for a prestigious track meet. His appeal to the state association was refused, though no meet official was in the area where the alleged foul occurred. A trial court injunction to allow participation was vacated by the state supreme court one day later.[69]
- The Ohio association adopted a rule making all out-of-state residents *forever* ineligible. A Kentucky resident who enrolled in a nearby Ohio Catholic school failed to convince the court of the arbitrariness of the rule or the deprivation of any constitutional rights.[70]

In 1938, the Supreme Court set the tone for the next cases.[71] Members of a high school football team were given a small, gold football worth a few dollars as an after-the-season award. This violation of an association rule caused ineligibility for one year, even though the awards were returned when the violation was discovered. The Oklahoma court said that if the rules or penalties were too harsh, the member school should change the rules and the controversies should stay out of the courtroom.

School and School-Related Organizations

Through the years, most controversies about school and school-related organizations have arisen at the post-secondary level. Official recognition of the student organization is usually the issue because it may give rights relating to use of school facilities and school channels of communication. Also, membership or participation in organizations not officially sanctioned by the school may cause the imposition of certain penalties, including removal from school, or ineligibility to hold certain offices or participate in other leadership activities.

The bulk of these cases arose during the last 50 years where state laws, board of education policies, and school rules were adopted to eliminate the morale and discipline problems caused by secret societies including fraternities and sororities at the secondary level.[72] Today's generally established law is that the state may prohibit the existence of, or membership in, secret societies if it chooses to do so. Very few of these policies have been judicially challenged in the last 20 years.

A Michigan school board policy forbade recognition of groups that advocated "controversial" ideas or stressed "one side" of issues. The decision as to which groups to recognize was left completely to the principal. His refusals to recognize the Mumford Committee to End Stress and the Mumford Young Socialist Alliance were challenged by several high school students claiming violation of First Amendment rights.

Following an analysis very similar to that conducted in the *Tinker* case, the court found no evidence of any past disruption of the orderly operation of the school or any plans for the future disruption of the school. The court ordered the student organizations be given official recognition, no penalties be imposed, and the defendants pay the plaintiffs' costs and reasonable attorney fees.[73]

Where constitutional rights are not obviously related to the decision or policy, the school boards are more likely to be judicially supported. An Ohio high school band was invited to participate in festivities connected with the Orange Bowl in Miami, Florida, during Christmas vacation. Expenses were to be borne completely by a band booster club. Based on a board policy prohibiting "long, expensive, out-of-state trips," the board refused to approve the trip.

Finding no constitutional right to participate in the activity and no evidence of lack of approval due to the exercise of some constitutional rights, the court dismissed the plaintiffs' complaint without a trial.[74] Interestingly, the judge suggested in his closing remarks that he could see no reasons why the band could not go without the board's approval since the board had indicated there would be no retaliation against anyone who went!

System/Building Rules and Eligibility

The point has been stressed repeatedly that courts are very reluctant to interfere with the policies and decisions of school officials. This is also true when the issue is the application of a variety of system policies and school rules.

Several challenges have been raised involving student participation in the graduation ceremony. The Casey (Iowa) High School graduation ceremonies of 1918 were marred by the refusal of several senior girls to wear caps and gowns as required by board policy. After some arguments over the poor fit of the caps, that requirement was eliminated. However, the young ladies still refused to wear the gowns provided because they smelled strongly of the formaldehyde with which they had been recently fumigated by the city health department.[75]

More recently, a North Carolina graduate wore brushed denim pants and a pair of dress boots to the graduation ceremony. The principal refused to allow him to participate in the ceremony because a previously-posted dress code required that males wear "dress pants as opposed to jeans," "shirts and ties," and "shoes and socks."

In both instances, the question of whether the student was entitled to a diploma was not the issue. The courts found that students had no constitutional right to walk across the stage, although they had met the graduation requirements and must be given their diplomas.[76] On the other hand, an Ohio student who had graduated during the school year sought permission to participate in the June graduation ceremonies. Although the system had no policy, she was told she could not participate. The Ohio court ruled in her favor and recognized "her right" to participate in the graduation ceremonies.[77] The court cited no legal authority to support the existence of such right.

Numerous challenges to school decisions affecting student eligibility for cocurricular activities relate to the application of rules against drinking alcoholic beverages or using drugs:

- A student who drank wine at home during the lunch hour was suspended from school, expelled from the National Honor Society, and forced to resign from a school pep organization.[78]
- Members of a school hockey team were suspended from the team for six weeks for violating known training rules. The incident occurred during a weekend trip out of town and while the team was staying at a hotel under the supervision of coaches and parents.[79]
- Several Nebraska athletes were removed permanently from the boys' and girls' basketball teams for drinking at a party in a private home during the basketball season in violation of coaches' rules.[80]
- A Nebraska student was suspended from the wrestling team for six weeks, and a Texas senior was removed from the National Honor Society after each was observed drinking in public.[81]

In all but the last case, *Warren v. National Association of Secondary School Principals,* the penalties imposed by the school officials were upheld.

What are some of the key legal messages gleaned from these cases? Following seemingly fair procedures to arrive at judgments and impose the penalties is important, as is evidence that the students had prior knowledge of the rules. Even when the initial stages of the procedures used to determine guilt are flawed, later efforts to remedy that defect may be adequate. The courts have applauded provisions for some internal administrative review opportunities. Admission of guilt by the student not only makes the administrator's or coach's job easier, but reduces the legal expectation relating to investigation and certainty of guilt.[82]

Why was the plaintiff successful in the *Warren* case? The constitution of the local National Honor Society chapter established certain procedures for removing a student from the organization, and the court concluded that school officials did not follow the due process rules they had established. (The National Association was not held liable for the chapter's actions.)

Earlier in this monograph, the United States Supreme Court case of *Goss v. Lopez* and the two-step due process analysis were discussed.[83] Several of the cases presented in this section occurred prior to the *Goss* opinion and contained legal analyses of due process that may be outdated. The 1975 date of *Goss v. Lopez* is pivotal in appreciating the legal meaning of property rights and procedural due process of law in school cases.

The nature and application of a rule is only part of the possible legal challenge. The extent of the penalty may also be challenged. Penalties have ranged from complete removal, to a 40-day suspension from cocurricular activities, to a four month's suspension from all cocurricular activities, to prohibiting a student to be a candidate for student council co-president.[84]

Courts are historically so reluctant to get involved in second-guessing school officials over the extent of the penalty, that in most cases cited above the plaintiffs did not even raise legal challenges to the extent of the penalty.

Many educators faced with resolving the difficult and emotional decisions required when rules are applied, look for ways to avoid making those hard decisions. One possible solution is to have some process whereby other student members of the organization make the decision about a fellow student's guilt or innocence and the extent of the penalty. A Tenth Circuit case focused on a constitution for the student government that had been adopted by the student body itself. The constitution imposed a good citizenship requirement for student council membership. Standing on that provision, the principal refused to allow a student to be a candidate for student council co-president because in the past, the student had written remarks criticizing the principal and the student council itself.

The court determined that because it was the *students'* constitution for a *student* organization, and because no state law or governmental action was actually involved in denying the student the opportunity to be a candidate, no basis existed for the case ever to come to federal court.[85] The court did not even discuss any question relating to a possible burden on the student's exercising his right of freedom of speech in his original written remarks by the later decision to prohibit his candidacy for office.

No other cases have supported leaving the decision to the student participants. Apart from the question of whether this case *would* be followed by any other courts, is the question of the educational and philosophical *appropriateness* of such administrative behavior. Student activities administrators should not take comfort in the outcome of this case.

The several cases just discussed offer instructive examples of how school officials can make the decisions that they believe are best for the system and for the individual and do so within the framework of law and fairness.

Buhlman v. Board of Education illustrates the belief that *good administration makes good law.*[86] In January 1980, the Suffern High School hockey team went to Saratoga, N.Y., for games on Friday and Saturday. Several parents accompanied the team and the coach. At about 11:00 p.m. and again at midnight, a bed check ensured that team members had obeyed the instructions to remain in their rooms with their lights out. Sometime after midnight, however, the coach heard a noise that led him to check on the team. He discovered players smoking marijuana and drinking beer.

The coach confronted each team member, and all except one admitted that they had been drinking or smoking. During the evening, the coach discussed the incident with the team captains and at least one parent. On Saturday he contacted the high school athletic director. They decided to take up the matter again on Monday morning. The coach also informed the parents present about what had taken place the previous evening.

On Monday, the principal, the assistant principals, the athletic director, and the hockey coach asked each boy:

1. Did you smoke?
2. Did you drink?
3. Did you participate in providing the beer?
4. Who should be exonerated?

The responses agreed with the facts that had been gleaned at the Saturday meeting of the coach and players.

The training rules and penalties were known by each of the athletes as they had been read and explained by the coach to the athletes.

The following day the principal notified each team member in writing that he would be suspended from the hockey team for six weeks based upon the rules and penalties that had previously been adopted. Soon thereafter, several parents offered the principal some alternatives for consideration. The principal indicated that he would consider them, but as the administrator, he had to make the decision. Ultimately, he stood by his original decision.

In a typical Fourteenth Amendment due process analysis, the court concluded that probably no protected property right was involved in participating in cocurricular activities. However, the court indicated it would consider what due process ought to be given. Upon consideration, the court concluded if any due process had been constitutionally required, it had surely been given by school officials. The coach's process was fair, and the principal's process was fair and appropriate to the circumstances. The plaintiff's complaint was dismissed by the court.

When in doubt about the process legally due, it is safest to provide some minimal procedures to demonstrate an effort at fairness.

Freedom of Religion and Speech

> Congress shall make no law respecting an establishment of religion, or prohibiting the free exercise thereof; or abridging the freedom of speech, or of the press; or the right of the people peaceably to assemble, and to petition the Government for a redress of grievances.[87]

The First Amendment explicitly protects the rights of speech, press, assembly, petitioning the government, no establishment of religion, and free exercise of religion. Additionally, the rights of free association and *privacy* have been found by the courts to be implied within the words and spirit of the amendment.

Many First Amendment issues have been raised in school litigation in the last two decades. In the early 1960s, freedom of religion was a great concern. By the late 1960s and early 1970s, freedom of speech and assembly were the bases for many legal challenges. In the early 1980s, freedom of religion had returned to the forefront.

In 1962-63 the United States Supreme Court ruled that the First Amendment prohibited the recitation of the Lord's Prayer and reading from the Bible in the public schools.[88] Since that time, innumerable efforts have been made by schools to avoid the full impact of those decisions. The consistent results of these cases, however, have been the continued prohibition of religious activities in public schools.

Interestingly, with the 1980s came suits challenging school board policies or decisions that did not allow religious activities, rather than suits to stop such activities. Two similar cases, *Johnson* and *Brandon,* arose over student requests to organize voluntary prayer or Bible study groups and be recognized as official school activities.[89] Whether before, during, or after school, the groups desired to hold voluntary meetings at the school with or without faculty supervision. In both instances, the administrators or school boards refused to grant permission or recognition.

Arguments based on the free exercise of religion clause were unsuccessful, as no evidence was offered to convince the court that students lacked other facilities or opportunities for exercising their religious beliefs. Additionally, the courts feared that in the school setting, the existence of such clubs would pressure the less orthodox to conform, or that approval would indicate a stamp of approval on such activities. To analyze any controversy relating to the establishment of religion clause, the Supreme Court asks three questions:

1. Does the activity have a secular purpose?
2. Does the principal or primary effect of the activity advance or inhibit religion?
3. Does the activity foster an excessive entanglement of government with religion?

While both courts concluded that the secular purpose of the activities (to encourage student participation) was acceptable under the First Amendment, both courts concluded that the answers to the second and third questions made the clubs unconstitutional. Obviously no other reason exists for having the clubs than to advance religion.

The courts have traditionally found that where public school buildings are used for student activities, faculty supervision is necessarily required and results in excessive governmental entanglement with religion. The courts upheld the decision of the board in both instances.

In 1983 a Pennsylvania federal district arrived at a decision completely opposite to those just discussed.[90] With essentially the same facts, the court adopted every argument unsuccessfully advanced in *Brandon* and *Johnson*. In view of the Supreme Court's recent refusal to review the *Brandon* decision, the long-term validity of this decision is doubtful.

At Adeline Senior High School in Texas, students sang or recited the Adeline School Prayer at athletic events, pep rallies, and graduation. Though said voluntarily and outside of regular school hours, the court found the prayer in violation of each of the guidelines previously identified.[91]

Courts have recognized some very narrow exceptions to this general prohibition on religious activities in the public schools. For example, a federal district court in Pennsylvania determined that the graduation ceremony had no impact on getting a diploma, and that participation in the ceremony was completely voluntary.[92] The court also distinguished the ceremonial nature of the occasion from religious activities that occur during the regular school day when attendance would be required.

Opening assemblies with a student-led prayer, conversely, violate both the free exercise and establishment clauses.[93]

Two recent cases demonstrate how boards of education can face freedom of religion questions in very different ways. On several occasions during the 1970s, the Lubbock (Texas) Independent School District received complaints about Christian evangelical religious activities during school assemblies. Evidence presented in court indicated the board knowingly ignored its own 1971 unofficial policy on the subject, and in 1979 it adopted a policy to allow the student-initiated activities which, in effect, helped to perpetuate the practices. Then, in 1980, the board adopted a policy that allowed voluntary meetings with adult supervision before and after school for educational, moral, religious, or ethical purposes.

Contrast the delaying tactics in that case with the efforts of the board of education of Sioux Falls, South Dakota. A suit had challenged the Christian religious nature of activities during the Christmas season. The board formed a committee of citizens and educators to develop a policy consistent with law to guide student activities during days of religious celebration.

In the former case, the board's intent to foster Christianity was obvious, and the plaintiff's challenge was successful. In the latter case, the challenge was unsuccessful and the board's efforts to resolve the problem fairly were praised by the court.[94]

One of the arguments often raised by those supporting religious activities in the public schools is that their freedom of speech and association is denied by the prohibition of such activities.[95] The courts have indicated that, as with all rights of Americans, time, place, and manner restrictions may be placed on the exercise of those rights. In these instances, students are certainly free to practice their religious beliefs outside the public school and at times other than during the school day.

In addition, the free speech that is protected by the Constitution and is so strongly supported in the *Tinker* case relates more especially to political speech. Thus, the court concluded that where freedom of religion and freedom of speech conflicted in the public school setting, separation of government from religion takes precedence over other considerations.

A New Jersey school board adopted a policy which effectively prohibited all Friday evening, Saturday daytime, and Sunday morning student activities except interscholastic sports, which the board had no control over as far as scheduling was concerned.

The policy was established so students would not be forced to choose between participating in school activities or participating in their own religious activities. The policy was also intended to ensure students equal opportunity to participate in these activities.

Drama Club members challenged the refusal to allow a Friday evening performance of a school play, since a double cast had been chosen for the play to allow more student participation. The court upheld the policy in the face of an establishment clause complaint because any advancement of religion was only incidental and the policy actually encouraged the exercise of religion free from government interference.[96]

An elementary school basketball coach enforced a rule which disallowed "suiting up" for the next game if the player missed a practice.[97] Two excuses were accepted: personal illness or death in the family. The policy was challenged because practice time conflicted with a weekly religion class. The court upheld the rule for several reasons: the religion class was not required; a non-conflicting class was readily available; the rule promoted important values of teamwork and responsibility to the group; no alternate, reasonable practice schedule existed; and any exception to the rule would actually benefit religion.

A Maryland case raised slightly different religious questions.[98] Beginning with the 1980-81 school year, the Allegheny County Public School System limited participation in its countywide music programs to full-time public school students. Previously, students in private schools had been allowed to participate in the program. These students claimed that government was burdening the free exercise of their religion by withdrawing participation privileges.

In rejecting such claims, the court determined that exercising the right to attend private schools necessarily reduced some of the rights to remain equally eligible for public school programs and this was no burden on the actual practice of religion.

Although no evidence indicated that serious problems had arisen in the past because of this dual involvement, the court accepted the board argument that the administrative complications could easily become overwhelming and, therefore, upheld the new policy.

Several cast members challenged the superintendent's decision not to allow the spring play, *Pippin,* to be presented. Even after changes had been made in the script, the superintendent concluded that the play placed too great an emphasis on the sexual behavior of the main character and the moral positions the play seemed to endorse. Students claimed a constitutional right to participate in a particular play under the First Amendment.

The court concluded that dramatic speech was not of the same nature as protected political speech. Just as students had no right to select the content of a senior history course, they had no right to choose a particular play to be presented;[99] such curriculum matters are left to educators and school boards. Further, the court was concerned that if the play were presented, the school would be seen as approving the behavior to which the board objected.

Another issue relating to sexual behavior was raised by a senior male student who wanted to take a male friend as his escort to the senior dinner-dance.[100] Based on the *Tinker* case, he claimed such action was an exercise of free speech and association. The principal denied his request for fear of some disruption or violence toward the students. However, because only one incident of previous disruption was offered as evidence, the court concluded that such undifferentiated fear or apprehension of disruptions was not enough to justify denying the student's free speech right. Finding this to be especially true because the dance was a voluntary social event and would take place away from the school environment, the court granted a preliminary injunction against the board's ruling.

Publications

The control of publications involves several kinds of factual situations:

1. In-school, student-produced publications
2. Out-of-school, student-produced publications with on-campus distribution
3. Out-of-school, student-produced publications with off-campus distribution
4. Out-of-school, non-student-produced publications with on-campus distribution by students
5. Out-of-school, non-student-produced publications with off-campus distribution by students.

A review of relevant cases suggests that none of these factual patterns involving who published, where distributed, or when distributed, always affects the outcome in the same way. Neither did the outcome hinge on whether someone had been punished rather than simply put in fear of reprisal for publishing or distributing.

Discussion of legal principles starts with the First Amendment and the *Tinker* case. Included within the First Amendment are guarantees of freedom of speech and freedom of the press. The *Tinker* case established that students do not shed their constitutional rights when they come to school. In fact, the freedom to express their views is a right that must be protected by public school officials although speech and press freedom may be limited in certain instances.

Numerous opinions of the Supreme Court, though not school-related, are appropriate to this discussion. Certain cases involve obscenity or requirements for approval from some governmental authority before publication or distribution.[101] The Supreme Court has never taken a case directly relating to publication and distribution by secondary students on or off campus, so the "law" is not especially easy to find or understand. Approximately 30 reported cases from the late '60s, '70s, and early '80s do not agree on results or legal theories, although judicial challenges by students succeeded almost 80 percent of the time.

From a review of the cases, what arguments raised by students in one or more cases have proved successful?

1. A school newspaper is a forum for the dissemination of ideas and is a peaceful, traditional method of expressing them.[102]
2. Content of ads may not be limited where the same content is allowed in news and editorial sections.[103]
3. The general authority of the school board over curriculum does not apply to student publications as they are a public forum and are not an official publication or statement of the school system.[104]
4. Freedom of the press protects distributing or selling as well as printing or writing.[105]
5. Anticipated disagreement over content from parents, teachers, administrators, board members, or other students is not a valid basis for limiting publication or distribution.[106]
6. While restrictions on time, place, and manner of distribution are allowable, such policies must not be so vague as to be misunderstood by a reasonable person.[107]
7. Time, place, and manner restrictions must specifically spell out the process for securing approval for distribution, must include an appeal process which is extremely brief, and must be evenhandedly applied to all.[108]
8. Policies limiting commercialism and solicitation of students must be evenhandedly enforced and may be of questionable application in controlling publications.[109]
9. Generalized fear or apprehension of disruption without evidence of actual disruption or evidence of imminent disruption may not be the basis for limiting publication or distribution.[110]
10. A decision to eliminate the publication and distribution of all student publications to avoid one undesirable publication is not an acceptable solution.[111]
11. Topics discussed and language used in publications may not be a basis for punishing a student where similar topics and language are found in the library and in required reading assignments.[112]
12. Claims of technical defects in a publication used as a basis to halt distribution will be closely reviewed.[113]
13. While school authority over students may sometimes extend to activities off campus, not during school time, and where there is a direct impact on the operation of the school, efforts to control publications published off campus and distributed before or after school off campus are probably beyond school authority.[114]

No one argument was raised in every case, nor was any argument successful in every case. However, the variety of successful arguments raised by students demonstrates the high degree of court receptivity to protecting freedom of the press as compared to other kinds of student behavior. Highlighting this protectiveness toward freedom of the press is a longstanding judicial view that securing approval *prior* to publication and distribution from governmental authority is highly disfavored. In this country, the general rule for any publications has been to allow publication and distribution and respond *after* the fact.

From the opposite perspective, what arguments have supported decisions of school boards and administrators to halt publication and distribution? These arguments have been drawn generally from non-school opinions of the United States Supreme Court where the Court identified examples of speech that were not protected by the First Amendment.

- Language and pictures which meet the complex definition of legal obscenity are not protected.[115]
- Advertising, so-called "commercial speech," traditionally does not get complete First Amendment protection.[116]
- Reasonably written policies and oral directions relating to time, place, and manner of distribution can include penalties for violations.[117]
- Governmental efforts to prevent psychological, emotional, or physical harm to its citizens may take precedence over First Amendment claims where convincing evidence is offered of actual harm or imminent likelihood of occurrence of such harm.[118]
- Student leaders and, perhaps, school administrators and staff, are not as unprotected from criticism as public officials in traditional positions open to public criticism.[119]

Full appreciation of the extent of control of publications by school officials requires consideration of these cases in an historical context. Most of them arose during or were related to the Vietnam War and were inspired by the activism of an earlier era. The zeal of students was met by an equal zeal of school officials, and resulted in situations that were handled in a more emotional manner, perhaps, than might have been desirable. The cases that went to court understandably represent more questionable legal behavior, and courts felt compelled to protect the First Amendment.

The controversial school topics of the early '80s are drugs and sex. These are subjects which look much less like free speech than did the words of student activists a decade earlier. Certainly, the law in this area has developed more definite boundaries at each end of the continuum from protected to unprotected behavior.

Controversies involving control of publications can be defused many times by the existence of formally-adopted school district policies. Whether a school system adopts an attitude of trying to exercise great control over student publications or an attitude of facilitating the intelligent exchange of ideas, adoption of policies *before* the heat of community controversy is generated is advised. The school setting is a special setting to the courts, and educators can monitor school publications and school grounds.

Summary

Athletic and activity associations have a massive impact on the principal and the operation of school activity programs. Eligibility rules based on age, attendance, address, and behavior are consistently upheld by courts. Dissatisfied school officials are told to work within the association to change any unfair rules.

Local schools and systems also retain broad authority to regulate activities and participants. Policies and rules which go far beyond association rules and which govern activities outside of association control may be adopted. Because most situations involving cocurricular activities do not involve federal constitutional rights, unhappy parents and students are consistently unsuccessful with judicial challenges.

Such judicially-recognized authority should not be interpreted to suggest no court will ever interfere. Plaintiffs often raise successful challenges in cases of infringement of basic, fundamental, constitutional rights by government, whether in the school activity setting or not.

Freedom of speech and freedom of the press are two of the most protected of our rights. Where those rights are obviously involved, as in the publications' cases, principals are unlikely to find judicial support.

Footnotes

1. Oklahoma High Sch. Ath. Ass'n. v. Bray, 321 F.2d 269 (10th Cir. 1963); Morrison v. Roberts, 82 P.2d 1023 (Okla. 1938); Albach v. Odle, 531 F.2d 983 (10th Cir. 1976).
2. 197 N.W.2d 555 (Iowa 1972).
3. United States Const. Amend. XIV; Oklahoma High Sch. Ath. Ass'n. v. Bray, 321 F.2d 269 (10th Cir. 1963); Rogers v. Board of Educ., 281 F. Supp. 39 (E.D. Ark. 1968).
4. Mitchell v. Louisiana High Sch. Ath. Ass'n., 430 F.2d 1155 (5th Cir. 1970); Lee v. Florida High Sch. Act. Ass'n., 291 So.2d 636 (Fla. App. 1974); Oklahoma High Sch. Ath. Ass'n. v. Bray, 321 F.2d 269 (10th Cir. 1963); Stock v. Texas Catholic Interscholastic League, 364 F. Supp. 362 (N.D. Tex. 1973).
5. *Contra* Duffley v. New Hampshire Interscholastic Ath. Ass'n., 446 A.2d 462 (N.H. 1982).
6. Hamilton v. Tennessee Secondary Sch. Ath. Ass'n., 552 F.2d 681 (6th Cir. 1976); Albach v. Odle, 531 F.2d 983 (10th Cir. 1976); Kulovitz v. Illinois High Sch. Ass'n., 462 F. Supp. 875 (N.D. Ill. 1978); Dallam v. Cumberland Valley Sch. Dist., 358 F. Supp. 358 (M.D. Pa. 1975); Sullivan v. University Interscholastic League, 599 S.W.2d 860 (Tex. Civ. App. 1980), *aff'd in part, rev'd in part,* 616 S.W.2d 170 (Tex. 1981); Menke v. Ohio High Sch. Ath. Ass'n., 441 N.E.2d 620 (Ohio 1981).
7. Sturrup v. Mahan, 305 N.E.2d 877 (Ind. 1974); Sullivan v. University Interscholastic League, 599 S.W.2d 860 (Tex. Civ. App. 1980), *aff'd in part, rev'd in part,* 616 S.W.2d 170 (Tex. 1981); United States *ex rel* Missouri High Sch. Act. Ass'n., 682 F.2d 147 (8th Cir. 1982).
8. Sullivan v. University Interscholastic League, 599 S.W.2d 860 (Tex. Civ. App. 1980), *aff'd in part, rev'd in part,* 616 S.W.2d 170 (Tex. 1981).
9. Sturrup v. Mahan, 305 N.E.2d 877 (Ind. 1974).
10. Crandall v. North Dakota High Sch. Act. Ass'n., 261 N.W.2d 921 (N.Dak. 1978); Mozingo v. Oklahoma Secondary Sch. Act. Ass'n., 575 P.2d 1379 (Okla. App. 1978); Quimby v. School Dist., 455 P.2d 1019 (Ariz. App. 1969); Kentucky High Sch. Ath. Ass'n. v. Hopkins City Bd. of Educ., 552 S.W.2d 685 (Ky. App. 1977)
11. Kriss v. Brown, 390 N.E.2d 193 (Ind. App. 1979).
12. Barnhorst v. Missouri State High Sch. Act. Ass'n., 504 F. Supp. 449 (W.D. Mo. 1980); Genusa v. Holy Cross College, Inc., 389 So.2d 908 (La. App. 1980); Chabert v. Louisiana High Sch. Ath. Ass'n., 323 So.2d 774 (La. 1975); Bruce v. South Carolina High Sch. League, 189 S.E.2d 817 (S.C. 1972); Cooper v. Oregon Sch. Act. Ass'n., 629 P.2d 386 (Oreg. App. 1981). *See generally* ABC League v. Missouri State High Sch. Ass'n., 530 F. Supp. 1033 (E.D. Mo. 1982), *rev'd sub nom.* United States *ex rel.* Missouri State High Sch. Act. Ass'n., 682 F.2d 147 (8th Cir. 1982).

13. Marino v. Waters, 220 So.2d 802 (La. App. 1969).
14. Walsh v. Louisiana High Sch. Ath. Ass'n., 616 F.2d 152 (5th Cir. 1980).
15. Compagno v. Nebraska Sch. Act. Ass'n., No. 77-L-192 (D. Nebr. Sept. 16, 1977).
16. Reed v. Nebraska Sch. Act. Ass'n., 341 F. Supp. 258 (D. Nebr. 1972).
17. Leffel v. Wisconsin Interscholastic Ath. Ass'n., 444 F. Supp. 1117 (E.D. Wis. 1978); Hoover v. Meiklejohn, 430 F. Supp. 164 (D. Colo. 1977); Carnes v. Tennessee Secondary Sch. Ath. Ass'n., 415 F. Supp. 569 (E.D. Tenn. 1976); Morris v. Michigan State Bd. of Educ., 472 F.2d 1207 (6th Cir. 1973); Brenden v. Independent Sch. Dist., 477 F.2d 1292 (8th Cir. 1973); Gilpin v. Kansas High Sch. Act. Ass'n., 377 F. Supp. 1233 (D. Kans. 1973); Haas v. South Bend Community Sch. Corp., 289 N.E.2d 495 (Ind. 1972); Bucha v. Illinois High Sch. Ass'n., 351 F. Supp. 69 (N.D. Ill. 1972); Ritacco v. Norwin Sch. Dist., 361 F. Supp. 930 (W.D. Pa. 1973).
18. 20 U.S.C. §1681 et seq. (1972); 45 C.F.R. §86.1-86.71 (1975).
19. 45 C.F.R. §86.41 (b) (1975).
20. Othen v. Ann Arbor Sch. Bd., 507 F. Supp. 1376 (E.D. Mich. 1981).
21. *See generally* North Haven Bd. of Educ. v. Bell 102 S. Ct. 1912 (1982).
22. O'Connor v. Board of Educ., 645 F.2d 578 (7th Cir. 1981).
23. O'Connor v. Board of Educ., 102 S.Ct. 641 (1981).
24. Darrin v. Gould, 540 P.2d 882 (Wash. 1975). *Accord* Pennsylvania v. Pennsylvania Interscholastic Ath. Ass'n., 334 A.2d 839 (Commw. Ct. Pa. 1975).
25. Forte v. Board of Educ., 431 N.Y.S.2d 321 (Sup. Ct. 1980); Mularadelis v. Haldane Central Sch. Bd., 427 N.Y.S.2d 458 (App. Div. 1980); Gomes v. Rhode Island Interscholastic League, 604 F.2d 733 (1st Cir. 1979); Petrie v. Illinois High Sch. Ass'n., 394 N.E.2d 855 (Ill. App. 1979); Clark v. Arizona Interscholastic Ass'n., 695 F.2d 1126 (9th Cir. 1982).
26. Attorney General v. Massachusetts Interscholastic Ath. Ass'n., 393 N.E.2d 284 (Mass. 1979).
27. Striebel v. Minnesota High Sch. League, 321 N.W.2d 400 (Minn. 1982).
28. Dodson v. Arkansas Act. Ass'n., 468 F. Supp. 394 (E.D. Ark. 1979); Jones v. Oklahoma Secondary Sch. Act. Ass'n., 453 F. Supp. 150 (W.D. Okla. 1977); Cape v. Tennessee Secondary Sch. Ath. Ass'n., 563 F.2d 793 (6th Cir. 1977).
29. Yellow Springs Exempted Village Sch. Dist. v. Ohio High Sch. Ath. Ass'n., 647 F.2d 651 (6th Cir. 1981).
30. 29 U.S.C. §794.
31. Spitaleri v. Nyquist, 345 N.Y.S.2d 878 (Sup. Ct. 1973); Colombo v. Sewanhaka Central High Sch. Dist., 383 N.Y.S.2d 518 (Sup. Ct. 1976).
32. Kampmeier v. Harris, 411 N.Y.S.2d 744 (App. Div. 1978).
33. Kampmeier v. Nyquist, 553 F.2d 269 (2nd Cir. 1977).
34. *Contra* Grube v. Bethlehem Area Sch. Dist., 550 F. Supp. 418 (E.D. Pa. 1982).
35. Wolff v. South Colonie Central Sch. Dist., 534 F. Supp. 758 (N.D. N.Y. 1982).
36. Doe v. Marshall, 622 F.2d 118 (5th Cir. 1980), *cert. denied,* 49 U.S.L.W. 3495 (May 18, 1981).
37. *See also* Quimby v. School Dist., 455 P.2d 1019 (Ariz. App. 1969).
38. *See generally* Laurenzo v. Mississippi High Sch. Act. Ass'n., 708 F.2d 1038 (5th Cir. 1983).
39. Lee v. Florida High Sch. Act. Ass'n., 291 So.2d 636 (Fla. App. 1974) and Florida High Sch. Act. Ass'n. v. Bryant, 313 So.2d 57 (Fla. App. 1975). *Contra* Robinson v. Illinois High Sch. Ass'n., 195 N.E.2d 38 (Ill. App. 1963); Mitchell v. Louisiana High Sch. Ath. Ass'n., 430 F.2d 1155 (5th Cir. 1970); Blue v. University Interscholastic League, 503 F. Supp. 1030 (N.D. Tex. 1980); Burtt v. Nassau County Ath. Ass'n., 421 N.Y.S.2d 172 (Sup. Ct. 1979); Dekalb County Sch. System v. White, 260 S.E.2d 853 (Ga. 1979); Mahan v. Agee, 652 P.2d 765 (Okla. 1982).
40. Missouri State High Sch. Act. Ass'n. v. Schoenlaub, 507 S.W.2d 354 (Mo. 1974).
41. Smith v. Crim, 240 S.E.2d 884 (Ga. 1977).
42. Robin v. New York State Pub. High Sch. Ath. Ass'n., 420 N.Y.S.2d 394 (App. Div. 1979).
43. Reisdorff v. Nebraska Sch. Act. Ass'n., No. 77-0-3 (D. Nebr. January 20, 1977); Caso v. New York State Pub. High Sch. Ath. Ass'n., 434 N.Y.S.2d 60 (App. Div. 1980).
44. Kubiszyn v. Alabama High Sch. Ath. Ass'n., 374 So.2d 256 (Ala. 1979).
45. Dumez v. Louisiana High Sch. Ath. Ass'n., 334 So.2d 494 (La. App. 1976).
46. Robin v. New York State High Sch. Ath. Ass'n., 420 N.Y.S.2d 394 (App. Div. 1979).
47. Kite v. Marshall, 661 F.2d 1027 (5th Cir. 1981), *cert. denied,* 50 U.S.L.W. 3982 (U.S. June 14, 1982); Art Gaines Baseball Camp, Inc. v. Houston, 500 S.W.2d 735 (Mo. App. 1973).
48. Hawksley v. New Hampshire Interscholastic Ath. Ass'n., 285 A.2d 797 (N.H. 1971).
49. Adamek v. Pennsylvania Interscholastic Ath. Ass'n., 426 A.2d 1206 (Commw. Ct. Pa. 1981).
50. Josephine County Sch. Dist. No. 7 v. Oregon Sch. Act. Ass'n., 515 P.2d 431 (Oreg. App. 1973).
51. Moreland v. Western Pa. Interscholastic Ath. League, 572 F.2d 121 (3rd Cir. 1978).
52. State v. Judges of the Ct. of Common Pleas, 181 N.E.2d 261 (Ohio 1962).
53. School Dist. of Harrisburg v. Pennsylvania Interscholastic Ath. Ass'n., 309 A.2d 353 (Pa. 1973).
54. Watkins v. Louisiana High Sch. Ath. Ass'n., 301 So.2d 695 (La. App. 1974).
55. Florida High Sch. Act. Ass'n. v. Bradshaw, 369 So.2d 398 (Fla. App. 1979).

56. Watkins v. Louisiana High Sch. Ath. Ass'n., 301 So.2d 695 (La. App. 1974).
57. Holy Cross College v. Louisiana High Sch. Ath. Ass'n., 632 F.2d 1287 (5th Cir. 1980).
58. University Interscholastic League v. Hardin-Jefferson Indep. S.D., 648 S.W.2d 770 (Tex. Civ. App. 1983).
59. Denis J. O'Connell High Sch. v. Virginia High Sch. League, 581 F.2d 81 (4th Cir. 1978), *cert. denied,* 440 U.S. 936 (1979); Valencia v. Blue Hen Conference, 476 F. Supp. 809 (D. Del. 1979).
60. Windsor Park Baptist Church v. Arkansas Act. Ass'n., 658 F.2d 618 (8th Cir. 1981).
61. Menora v. Illinois High Sch. Ass'n., 527 F. Supp. 637 (N.D. Ill. 1981), *vacated,* 683 F.2d 1030 (7th Cir. June, 1982).
62. Board of Educ. v. Regional Bd. of Sch. Trustees, 405 N.E.2d 495 (Ill. App. 1980).
63. Florida High Sch. Act. Ass'n. v. Thomas, 409 So.2d 245 (Fla. App. 1982).
64. Id. at 247.
65. Baltic Indep. Sch. Dist. v. South Dakota High Sch. Act. Ass'n., 362 F. Supp. 780 (D. S.Dak. 1973).
66. Spain v. Louisiana High Sch. Ath. Ass'n., 398 So.2d 1386 (La. 1981).
67. Anderson v. South Dakota High Sch. Ath. Ass'n., 247 N.W.2d 481 (S.Dak. 1976).
68. Georgia High Sch. Ass'n. v. Waddell, 285 So.2d 7 (Ga. 1981).
69. Snow v. New Hampshire Interscholastic Ath. Ass'n., 449 A.2d 1223 (N.H. 1982).
70. Menke v. Ohio High Sch. Ath. Ass'n., 441 N.E.2d 620 (Ohio App. 1981).
71. Morrison v. Roberts, 82 P.2d 1023 (Okla. 1938).
72. Wayland v. Board of Sch. Directors, 86 P. 642 (Wash. 1906); Bradford v. Board of Educ., 121 P. 929 (Calif. App. 1912); Coggins v. Board of Educ., 28 S.E.2d 527 (N.C. 1944); Hughes v. Caddo Parish Sch. Bd., 57 F. Supp. 508 (W.D. La. 1945); Holroyd v. Eibling, 188 N.E.2d 797 (Ohio App. 1962); Robinson v. Sacramento City Unified Sch. Dist., 53 Cal. Rptr. 781 (Calif. App. 1966). *Contra* Wright v. Board of Educ., 246 S.W. 43 (Mo. 1922).
73. Dixon v. Beresh, 361 F. Supp. 253 (E.D. Mich. 1973).
74. Park Hills Music Club, Inc. v. Board of Educ., 512 F. Supp. 1040 (S.D. Ohio 1981).
75. Valentine v. Independent Sch. Dist., 183 N.W. 434 (Iowa 1921).
76. Fowler v. Williamson, 448 F. Supp. 498 (W.D. N.C. 1978).
77. Clark v. Board of Educ., 367 N.E.2d 69 (Ohio C.P. 1977).
78. Ector County Indep. Sch. Dist. v. Hopkins, 518 S.W.2d 576 (Tex. Civ. App. 1974).
79. Buhlman v. Board of Educ., 436 N.Y.S.2d 192 (Sup. Ct. 1981).
80. Braesch v. De Pasquale, 265 N.W.2d 842 (Nebr. 1978).
81. French v. Cornwell, 276 N.W.2d 216 (Nebr. 1979); Warren v. National Ass'n. of Secondary Sch. Principals, 375 F. Supp. 1043 (N.D. Tex. 1974).
82. Braesch v. De Pasquale, 265 N.W.2d 842 (Nebr. 1978); McNaughton v. Circleville Bd. of Educ., 345 N.E.2d 649 (Ohio C.P. 1974); Quinlan v. University Place Sch. Dist., 660 P.2d 329 (Wash. App. 1983).
83. *See supra* p. 10.
84. Bernstein v. Menard, 557 F. Supp. 90 (E.D. Va. 1982); Davis v. Central Dauphin Sch. Dist., 466 F. Supp. 1259 (M.D. Pa. 1979); McNaughton v. Circleville Bd. of Educ., 345 N.E.2d 649 (Ohio C.P. 1974); Pegram v. Nelson, 469 F. Supp. 1134 (M.D. N.C. 1979); Palacios v. Foltz, 441 F.2d 1196 (10th Cir. 1971).
85. Palacios v. Foltz, 441 F.2d 1196 (10th Cir. 1971).
86. 436 N.Y.S.2d 192 (Sup. Ct. 1981).
87. U.S. Const. Amend. I.
88. Engel v. Vitale, 370 U.S. 421 (1962); School Dist. of Abington Township v. Schempp, 374 U.S. 203 (1963).
89. Johnson v. Huntington Beach Union Sch. Dist., 137 Cal. Rptr. 43 (Calif. App. 1977); Brandon v. Board of Educ., 635 F.2d 971 (2nd Cir. 1980), *cert. denied,* 454 U.S. 1123 (1981).
90. Bender v. Williamsport Area Sch. Dist., 563 F. Supp. 697 (M.D. Pa. 1983).
91. Doe v. Adeline Indep. Sch. Dist., 563 F. Supp. 883 (S.D. Tex. 1982).
92. Wood v. Mount Lebanon Township Sch. Dist., 342 F. Supp. 1293 (W.D. Pa. 1972).
93. Collins v. Chandler Unified Sch. Dist., 470 F. Supp. 959 (D. Ariz. 1979), *modified,* 644 F.2d 759 (9th Cir. 1981).
94. Lubbock Civil Liberties Union v. Lubbock Indep. Sch. Dist., 669 F.2d 1038 (5th Cir. 1982), *cert. denied,* 103 S.Ct. 800 (1983); Florey v. Sioux Falls Sch. Dist., 619 F.2d 1311 (8th Cir.), *cert. denied,* 449 U.S. 987 (1980).
95. Brandon v. Board of Educ., 635 F.2d 971 (2nd Cir. 1980), *cert. denied,* 454 U.S. 1123 (1981).
96. Student Members of the Playcrafters v. Board of Educ., 424 A.2d 1192 (App. Div. 1981).
97. Keller v. Gardner Community Consol. Grade Sch. Dist., 552 F. Supp. 512 (N.D. Ill. 1982).
98. Thomas v. Allegany County Bd. of Educ., 443 A.2d 622 (Md. Ct. Spec. App. 1982). *See* Synder v. Charlotte Pub. Sch. Dist., 333 N.W.2d 542 (Mich. App. 1983).
99. Seyfried v. Walton, 512 F. Supp. 235 (D. Del. 1981), *aff'd.,* 668 F.2d 214 (3rd Cir. 1982).

100. Fricke v. Lynch, 491 F. Supp. 381 (D. R.I. 1980).
101. Miller v. California, 413 U.S. 15 (1973); Roth v. United States, 354 U.S. 476 (1957); Near v. Minnesota, 283 U.S. 697 (1931).
102. Zucker v. Panitz, 299 F. Supp. 102 (S.D. N.Y. 1969); Bayer v. Kinzler, 383 F. Supp. 1164 (E.D. N.Y. 1974).
103. Hernandez v. Hanson, 430 F. Supp. 1154 (D. Nebr. 1977); Zucker v. Panitz, 299 F. Supp. 102 (S.D. N.Y. 1969).
104. Gambino v. Fairfax County Sch. Bd., 564 F.2d 157 (4th Cir. 1977).
105. Quarterman v. Byrd, 453 F.2d 54 (4th Cir. 1971); Bright v. Los Angeles Unified Sch. Dist., 556 P.2d 1090 (Calif. 1976).
106. Shanley v. Northeast Indep. Sch. Dist., 462 F.2d 960 (5th Cir. 1972); Thomas v. Board of Educ., 607 F.2d 1043 (2nd Cir. 1979).
107. Fujishima v. Board of Educ., 460 F.2d 1355 (7th Cir. 1972); Scoville v. Board of Educ., 425 F.2d 10 (7th Cir. 1970); Shanley v. Northeast Indep. Sch. Dist., 462 F.2d 960 (5th Cir. 1972).
108. Koppell v. Levine, 347 F. Supp. 456 (E.D. N.Y. 1972); Pliscou v. Holtville Unified Sch. Dist., 411 F. Supp. 842 (S.D. Calif. 1976); Eisner v. Stamford Bd. of Educ., 440 F.2d 803 (2nd Cir. 1971); Nitzberg v. Parks, 525 F.2d 378 (4th Cir. 1975); Leibner v. Sharbaugh, 429 F. Supp. 744 (E.D. Va. 1977); Baughman v. Freienmuth, 478 F.2d 1345 (4th Cir. 1973); Fujishima v. Board of Educ., 460 F.2d 1355 (7th Cir. 1972); Quarterman v. Byrd, 453 F.2d 54 (4th Cir. 1971).
109. Peterson v. Board of Educ., 370 F. Supp. 1208 (D. Nebr. 1973).
110. Riseman v. School Committee, 439 F.2d 148 (1st Cir. 1971); Koppell v. Levine, 347 F. Supp. 456 (E.D. N.Y. 1972); Bayer v. Kinzler, 383 F. Supp. 1164 (E.D. N.Y. 1974); Scoville v. Board of Educ., 425 F.2d 10 (7th Cir. 1970); Quarterman v. Byrd, 453 F.2d 54 (4th Cir. 1971).
111. Pliscou v. Holtville Unified Sch. Dist., 411 F. Supp. 842 (S.D. Calif. 1976); Vail v. Board of Educ., 354 F. Supp. 592 (D. N.H. 1973); Sullivan v. Houston Indep. Sch. Dist., 475 F.2d 1071 (5th Cir. 1973).
112. Vought v. Van Buren Pub. Schools, 306 F. Supp. 1388 (E.D. Mich. 1969).
113. Reineke v. Cobb County Sch. Dist., 484 F. Supp. 1252 (N.D. Ga. 1980).
114. Scoville v. Board of Educ., 425 F.2d 10 (7th Cir. 1970); Fujishima v. Board of Educ., 460 F.2d 1355 (7th Cir. 1972); Thomas v. Board of Educ., 607 F.2d 1043 (2nd Cir. 1979).
115. Vought v. Van Buren Pub. Schools, 306 F. Supp. 1388 (E.D. Mich. 1969).
116. Williams v. Spencer, 622 F.2d 1200 (4th Cir. 1980); Katz v. McAulay, 438 F.2d 1058 (2nd Cir. 1971).
117. Graham v. Houston Indep. Sch. Dist., 335 F. Supp. 1164 (S.D. Tex. 1970); Sullivan v. Houston Indep. Sch. Dist., 475 F.2d 1071 (5th Cir. 1973); Baker v. Downey City Bd. of Educ., 307 F. Supp. 517 (C.D. Colo. 1969).
118. Trachtman v. Anker, 563 F.2d 512 (2nd Cir. 1977), *cert. denied,* 435 U.S. 925 (1978); Williams v. Spencer, 622 F.2d 1200 (4th Cir. 1980).
119. Frasca v. Andrews, 463 F. Supp. 1043 (E.D. N.Y. 1979).

Chapter III

Liability for Injuries

If any legal topic seems especially difficult to understand, it is tort law—that area of law that involves personal injuries. Unfortunately, nothing can prevent successful tort suits against institutions and employees, partly because this area of the law is intentionally open-ended to provide injured persons an opportunity to develop new theories by which to seek compensation for their injuries.

While knowledge of the current rules will not necessarily prevent a suit from being filed, such knowledge can be used to diminish the likelihood of *successful* suits.

What follows is an overview of general rules relating to tort liability that are most likely to arise from student activities. A comprehensive treatment of all aspects of tort law will not be developed here; an individual state's common law and statutes must be researched to determine the likely results of specific situations. This is the job of an attorney.

Although actual cases are offered as representative examples, slightly different facts could cause a *very* different result. Understanding the philosophy and principles of tort law is more important than being able to identify case results. The old adage, ''An ounce of prevention is worth a pound of cure,'' applies to this subject.

Our legal system is often characterized as ''Anglo-American'' because its roots extend hundreds of years back into British jurisprudence. The development of tort law—as well as criminal, contract, or property law—can be traced historically through opinions of English judges to the 1200s and 1300s. Tort law is essentially a result of judicial decisions—common law—rather than statutory or legislative law.

Tort law was developed to regulate the relations between two parties when one party claimed to have been injured as a result of the intentional or accidental action of the other party. Historically, the first torts involved trespassing on property or taking another's goods. Later, torts involved injuries that were intentional and were potential causes of blood-letting within the society as one party sought revenge. As society became more insistent on regulating individual efforts to protect one's rights, more torts appeared. As social mores change, those behaviors classified as torts may change, and other behaviors may become regulated.

The main purpose of tort law is to make the injured party whole again through assessment of monetary damages as a remedy. For what injuries can damages be recovered? Medical and hospital expenses, lost earnings, and pain and suffering associated with the injury are compensable. These may be expenses accrued prior to the trial and projected for the future. One's estate may also recover for a person's wrongful death, and parents or a spouse may be awarded compensation for loss of a loved one.

Since the focus of this chapter is student activities-related torts, the discussion will not focus on intentional torts, as they are unlikely to arise in this setting. Some mention will be made of the one intentional tort to arise in this context—assault and battery.[1] This tort involves intent to bring about harmful or offensive contact to the plaintiff, whether maliciously or as a practical joke.

A seventh-grade football coach was displeased with a student's blocking performance. After yelling at the boy, the coach knocked him to the ground by striking his helmet, then grabbed the boy's face mask. The 12-year-old weighed 115 pounds; the coach was 5′11″ and weighed 195 pounds. After eight days in the hospital and several months of recuperation, the student sued the coach for assault and battery.

The court concluded that to "fire the student up" rather than to enforce proper instructional commands was not the behavior of a reasonable coach.[2] The Texas appellate court remanded the case to the lower court for a new trial to cure earlier procedural faults.

The rest of this chapter concerns the unintentional tort of *negligence*. Prevention of successful negligence suits requires thoughtful cooperation of all those administering and conducting student activity programs.

Throughout any discussion of negligence, one concept—the "reasonable man"—consistently reappears. Remember that principles of tort law arose to allow society to tell its members how to behave toward each other. Through its judges, society devised the idea of the "reasonable man," or as more modern courts may say, the "reasonable person."

Negligence may be defined as "the doing of that thing which a reasonably prudent person would not have done, or the failure to do that thing which a reasonably prudent person would have done in like or similar circumstances; it is the failure to exercise that degree of care and prudence that reasonably prudent persons would have exercised in like or similar circumstances."[3]

Although written in 1930, these words well describe the legal concept of the reasonable person:

> He is an ideal, a standard, the embodiment of all those qualities which we demand of a good citizen. . . . He is the one who invariably looks where he is

> going, and is careful to examine the immediate foreground before he executes a leap or a bound; who neither star gazes nor is lost in meditation when approaching trapdoors or the margin of a dock; . . . who never mounts a moving omnibus and does not alight from any car while the train is in motion . . . and will inform himself of the history and habits of a dog before administering a caress; . . . who never drives his ball until those in front of him have definitely vacated the putting green which is his own objective; who never from one year's end to another makes excessive demand upon his wife, his neighbors, his servants, his ox, or his ass; . . . who never swears, gambles, or loses his temper; who uses nothing except in moderation, and even while he flogs his child is meditating only on the golden mean.[4]

How is the reasonable-person standard actually applied in a tort case? After all the evidence is presented, the judge gives the jury instructions to compare the behavior of the defendant to the behavior of a reasonable man. The latter's behavior varies from case to case, depending on the circumstances, but the reasonable man is presumed to possess these characteristics:

- The physical attributes of the defendant
- Normal intelligence
- Normal perception and memory
- A minimum level of information and experience common to the community
- Such superior skill and knowledge as the defendant has or holds himself out as having.[5]

If the defendant is five feet tall and weighs 105 pounds, the reasonable person is five feet tall and weighs 105 pounds. Even if the defendant is mentally handicapped, theoretically the presumption is normal intelligence, normal perception and memory, and minimum information and experience. Because this level of information and experience is based on the community, expectations of the reasonable person are likely to differ in rural Nebraska and San Francisco.

Finally, if the person accused of causing the injury claims to have special skills or knowledge, e.g., doctor, lawyer, athletic trainer, or water safety instructor, then the person is held to a higher level of behavior based on that claim.

The simple principle to remember about negligence is: "Always behave as a reasonably prudent person in your position would behave." When deciding whether to have the football team run an additional lap around the field after a three-hour practice in 95° weather, the coach should ask himself whether a reasonable person would do so under the same circumstances.

Obviously, knowing in advance what a reasonably prudent person would do in any given situation is impossible, and judges are well aware of this. For that reason, considerable judicial effort has been expended trying to develop some kind of test to determine whether or not the defendant's behavior meets the standard of the reasonably prudent person.

One such test, the foreseeability test, though not always applied, has been used in many negligence cases and may be useful to educators charged with responsibility for the health, welfare, and safety of students. As stated by Justice Cardoza in one of the most famous of negligence cases, "The risk reasonably to be perceived defines the duty to be obeyed.''[6] In other words, was the risk of injury in a given situation foreseeable by a person in the defendant's position?

Note that the law does not require the plaintiff to show that the specific injury which occurred was foreseeable in order for liability to be assigned, only that risks of that general type were foreseeable. On the other hand, the law does not require the defendant to assume impractical and unreasonable burdens to prevent all possible harm.[7]

Finally, the foreseeability test takes into account the age and presumed wisdom of the students to whom the duty is owed. Obviously, the younger or less mentally competent the student, the greater that duty will be. Even in the case of very young children, however, the courts will not impose the responsibility of an insurer on the school or its personnel. As stated by the court in a case in which a student drowned while on an excursion:

> It appears to us that [the principal] had fulfilled his duty when he gave appropriate instructions and specified certain conditions under which the trip might be taken. He was guilty of no negligence. . . . The duties of a principal of a school are manifold and he cannot be at all places at all times. . . . ''[8]

Who Gets Sued for Negligence?

The System, The Institution, The Board of Education

Suing the person or entity with the ''deepest pocket,'' otherwise known as the ''you-can't-get-blood-out-of-a-turnip'' theory, dictates to the plaintiff's attorney exactly whom to sue. To sue those with the most monetary resources, whether due to wealth, insurance, or taxing authority, is most beneficial. The best facts in the world are useless if the party whom you are suing has no resources. Thus, the plaintiff tries to sue the system or the institution.

The flaw in this logic, however, comes with the traditional common law doctrine of *sovereign* or *governmental immunity*—a rule that state governmental institutions (and their treasuries) are *not* liable for torts committed by board members, officers, and employees. Where this doctrine still exists, a lawsuit may not be brought against the state, regardless of right or wrong.

Recently, the doctrine of sovereign immunity has eroded and, in many instances, been eliminated completely in some of the 50 states. Usually, this has been accomplished by legislation, but in some cases where the state legislature would not act, the courts have.[9] One must review the judicial decisions and statutes of any particular state to determine the exact status of sovereign immunity.[10]

What about suing individual board members as ''official representatives'' of the system as a way to avoid the immunity doctrine? While some courts not favorably disposed to sovereign immunity may allow this, most courts would see the true intent of the suit and dismiss the case.

What about suits against nonpublic institutions? For many of the same policy reasons that governmental immunity developed, a comparable immunity for charitable institutions arose. But "charitable immunity," as it is called, has been eliminated or seriously reduced in almost every state. Thus, private and parochial schools can generally be sued for unintentional torts, such as negligence.[11]

Board Member, Superintendent, Principal, Athletic Director

Consideration of suit against these people must come from two points of view: suing them as official representatives of the system and suing them as individuals. When the individual is merely a conduit through which the system acted, and the intent of the suit is to get at the public treasury, courts supportive of governmental immunity would generally bar the suit.

What about suing these people as individuals? The common law doctrine of sovereign immunity that protects the institution itself does *not* usually extend to individual board members or employees when sued as individuals. However, these educators may not be held liable for the acts or omissions of their subordinates. Because they are usually one step personally removed from direct contact with student injury, successful suits can only be based on instances of inadequate maintenance of facilities and equipment or inadequate supervision of staff.[12]

Some states, like Illinois, have adopted statutes which focus on whether or not the state's immunity extends to employees and officers.[13] (For more detailed analysis of principal liability for negligence, see NASSP's *Legal Memoranda,* September and December 1980.)

Coach, Sponsor, Teacher, Other Participants

Because coaches, sponsors, and teachers are in direct contact with pupils, and thus most intimately connected with injuries, these people are the most obvious targets for tort suits. What about coaches, sponsors, and teachers in private, nonpublic institutions? They are liable for their acts at home or on the street.

The list of potential defendants also includes other activity participants, spectators, retailers and manufacturers, auditorium and field owners, and the state athletic/activity association.[14]

Before principals panic at the apparent openness to tort suit, the explanations that follow about the elements necessary to successfully prove any negligence action and the numerous defenses that are available should be considered. The law has raised significant barriers to the successful conduct of the tort suit against schools, administrators, and employees. For negligence to be found, one person must take an unreasonable risk, thereby causing injury to another. The question, "was an unreasonable risk taken in this situation?" is answered by determining how the reasonable person would have behaved in the same or similar circumstances.

Negligence

Proving a Claim

All torts require the plaintiff to prove that certain legal requirements are present. Proving a claim of negligence requires proof of four elements: duty, breach of duty, proximate cause, and actual injuries.

A legal ''duty'' exists when one person's relationship to another is such that it places an obligation upon him to exercise at least ordinary care that the other person is not injured. To determine whether such an obligation exists in a particular case, three questions must be answered:

- What is the nature/extent of the relationship?
- If there is a duty, to whom is it owed?
- Who owes the duty?

Defendants fight ''tooth and nail'' over the existence of a duty because the judge, not a soft-hearted jury, decides the question.

Being a sponsor, coach, teacher, or principal generally creates the necessary relationship with students to establish a legal duty. Sponsoring a wrestling team, approving high school clubs, and inviting spectators to attend a football game create a duty.[15] Courts in some states determine whether duty is owed by labeling the individual making a claim as a trespasser, licensee, or invitee.[16] These labels, with definitions relatively meaningless to the nonlawyer, are then used to determine the nature of the defendant's duty, if any.

The hardest problem is identifying the nature and extent of the duty. Duty changes with the facts and circumstances. The key appears to be the risks foreseeable in a particular activity. A teacher in a science laboratory or in the industrial education shop must deal with inherently great risks of injury. A campus with heavy through-traffic or high crime forces a higher duty upon the principal and school board toward students.

The following school activity situations were ones in which courts found educators to have a legal duty:

- Walking Special Olympics team members (I.Q. of 52) from the school to a city gym three blocks away via a busy street[17]
- Condoning off-campus initiation and hazing activities by school clubs[18]
- Installing a glass panel located six feet from the end of a basketball court, especially after one had been previously broken[19]
- Taking a six-year-old to the beach.[20]

Conversely, courts found no duty to exist in the following instances:

- Transporting football players to a nearby town for free physical examinations[21]
- Extending the backstop for the baseball diamond beyond the most

dangerous area and beyond seating for the expected crowd[22]

- Providing crowd control along the sidelines for third team football games[23]
- Choosing not to provide buses for cocurricular activities when the state law gave the board discretion to decide[24]
- Purchasing long-term disability insurance for football players[25]
- Repairing an entrance ramp to a baseball field when there was no history of a problem and no notice when a problem with slipperiness developed[26]
- Failing to send a recommendation for an athletic scholarship to a university[27]
- Having guards to prevent assaults at a city museum when none had been previously reported.[28]

The question of duty is really a question of whom can the plaintiff successfully sue and whether a system is liable for the actions of its employees. Where governmental immunity is not present, courts generally find the system liable for its employees' negligent acts when committed during the course of duty.[29] Intentional torts or criminal acts do not cause liability for the system, but do cause liability for the individual.[30]

Once a duty has been demonstrated, the plaintiff is required to show that the defendant did not carry out his duty to act as a reasonably prudent person toward the plaintiff. Reference must be made to the reasonable person concept. The question is asked: "Under the same or similar circumstances, would a reasonably prudent educator have acted as the educator did in this case?" This is probably the most litigated element of negligence.

The breach of duty element requires sifting evidence to arrive at facts which describe the defendant's behavior. Some of the following cases will seem to have more obvious breaches than others:

- A 16-year-old collapsed after an hour-and-a-half football practice session which concluded with wind sprints. He displayed all the signs of heat stroke and exhaustion. The first-aid treatment given was not only ill-chosen, but medical testimony suggested it was exactly opposite of that needed. Worst of all, the coaches denied the player access to medical treatment for almost two hours. Never regaining consciousness, the boy died later that evening.[31]
- In constructing a gymnasium, St. Mary's School allowed glass panels to be erected within six feet of a basketball court endline.[32] Two of the four panels were previously broken yet no effort was made to alleviate the danger.
- A shop teacher-Boy Scout leader sent student volunteers to get rocks for a fireplace at a scout camp.[33] The students were to drive a school truck which had no hood, only part of a windshield, and a portion of the floorboards. A homemade electrical device was used to start the truck, and the motor pumped oil out onto the passengers. The teacher had given the students no warnings or coping instructions.
- As part of the traditional lettermen's club initiation, the initiates were subjected to an electrical shock.[34] The homemade rheostat

used was quickly and crudely made. The wet floor conditions added to the danger when electricity was used. The coach did not test all the wires. One boy received a severe shock, and the next boy to be "initiated" was electrocuted.

- An Illinois school failed to provide any helmets or faceguards for a powderpuff football game played at the high school stadium[35] and the teacher-coaches did not instruct the players to find and use either piece of equipment.
- A Massachusetts school, through its coach, chose not to purchase one-piece hockey helmets despite the fact that the coach knew they were safer than the three-piece helmet in use. (The manufacturer and retailer were found to have breached their duties to construct and sell safe products.)[36]
- Lack of supervision is a common demonstration of breach of duty in school activity cases. A teacher and six adults took 35 elementary and preschool children to the beach. Four children climbed onto a large log, and posed for a picture that the teacher took. With her back to the ocean, the teacher did not see the large wave that surged onto the beach. The wave caused the log to be buoyed, and the children fell off. When the water receded, the log settled on top of one child and crushed him.

  Although no such violent wave action had occurred before that time, the court concluded that the possibility of such action was common knowledge in the area and found that the teacher had breached her duty to supervise.[37]
- Members of a senior class met at a city park on a Saturday to have pictures taken for the school yearbook.[38] The school had approved the activity and two teachers were assigned as supervisors. Two students had received permission to have their pictures taken while on their motorcycles. In the course of the morning, and with no evidence offered that the cyclists were "goofing off," a youngster walking nearby was hit and injured.
- In February 1972, the St. Paul Public Schools decided that senior high school students should attend a showing of "KING, A Filmed Record, Montgomery to Memphis" at a downtown theater. One teacher was assigned to each 35 students, but the evidence indicated a "lack of supervision and organization" of the students, as students were disruptive.[39]
- The head coach of a Special Olympics basketball team was allowed to conduct practice during her regular physical education period. To give the team experience in playing on a wood rather than a dirt court, she arranged to use a city gymnasium three blocks away. The assistant coach and 10-11 boys left for the gymnasium before the head coach was ready, though she gave permission for their departure. The chosen route required walking, rather than driving, across an extremely busy main street and crossing at a corner without a stop light. One boy was struck and killed by an auto. The court found breaches in the failure to use buses or cars, provide enough supervi-

sory personnel, give adequate safety instructions, choose the safest route, and maintain control of the students.[40]

- To make the play, "Li'l Abner," more realistic, the teacher chose to use shotguns and live ammunition—minus the shot, wadding, and powder. Not only did her choice of props seem "highly questionable" to the court, but the teacher admitted she never supervised or inspected the ammunition.[41]

Three more cases, although not finally resolved (as the appellate courts remanded the cases for trial), contribute to appreciation of the breach of duty concept.

An Illinois high school athletic director knew that kids always "horsed around" behind the bleachers at football games,[42] so he hired off-duty policemen and teachers to keep order. He admitted that the kids would return after the adults left. An elderly spectator was injured when one of the kids collided with her.

In Michigan, pre-season weight lifting sessions were held for the football team in a room at the school.[43] The plaintiff alleged that the principal and athletic director failed to supervise the coaches by allowing them to push students to lift weights beyond their limits. Also, no safety rules were enforced and the room was alleged to be poorly ventilated, causing dangerous, excessive perspiration.

A teacher was assigned as sponsor of a student club which had a history of violating school board regulations. The sponsor was not present for the planning meeting for the initiation or for the initiation session during which an injury occurred. The court spoke critically of the "see no evil, hear no evil" attitude displayed by the principal and sponsor.

Obviously the variety of possible breaches of duty is endless. Contrary to popular presumptions, the following cases demonstrate that plaintiffs do not always win. Losses may be attributed to poorly prepared cases, technical problems, and conflicting evidence.[44]

The preponderance of the evidence may also demonstrate that the defendant fulfilled his or her duty as far as reasonably possible. For example, an Oregon football coach used an extensive fitness program to get his players in proper physical condition.[45] He provided protective equipment and taught them how to run, tackle, and be tackled. He taught them proper techniques to make best use of their protective equipment, though he never explicitly told the players not to use their heads as battering rams.

It is often assumed that leaving students without supervision automatically results in liability in case of injury. This is not so. A drama teacher left five high school seniors alone in the school auditorium to work on scenery for the school play.[46] A female student was injured when she fell through an open hatchway on stage, after the lights went out. The teacher was not found to have breached her duty because, for one thing, the loss of lights was not reasonably foreseeable.

Proximate cause, or legal cause, is the relationship that must be found to exist between the behavior and the claimed injury to justify a finding of liability. Proximate cause may also be defined as "that which, in a natural and continuous sequence, unbroken by any efficient intervening cause, produces the injury, and without which the result would not have occurred.''[47] The legal emphasis is upon whether the defendant's behavior ultimately caused the injury or whether it came about through chance or the actions of another person.

When this element of negligence is debated, the reason is usually that the natural and continuous sequence of events was broken by an alleged ''intervening cause.'' In this event, the defendant attempts to prove that his act was *not* the proximate cause of the injury because an intervening act superseded his act as the cause of the injury.[48]

Typically, this means the intervening act comes later in time and replaces the original breach as the cause of the injury. When such an intervening act is *foreseeable,* of course, the act then does *not* replace the plaintiff's behavior as the legal cause.

The earlier-described case involving attendance at the movie, represents foreseeable behavior by outside parties.[49] Not only did racial tension exist in other schools in St. Paul as well as the plaintiff's high school, obscene racial comments were made during the movie. The student testified that ''significant tension'' existed in the theater after the movie. In finding for the plaintiff, the jury recognized that some violence or injury (slashed wrist and stolen purse) was to be expected and steps should have been taken to protect students.

Prior to a play performance, the stage crew discovered that they had no dry ice for the fog-making machine.[50] Someone decided the contents of a fire extinguisher would create a suitable effect. A last minute test proved satisfactory. The machine was left plugged in though no thermostat was present. The explosion from the heated and ever-expanding gas demonstrated an ''elementary concept of science'' and was completely foreseeable.

Proximate cause is sometimes relatively easy to find. The lettermen's club's use of electric shock as part of the initiation ceremony is an obvious example.[51] Similarly obvious is the case in which the coaches kept a player suffering from heat stroke away from medical attention for two hours and used improper first-aid treatment.[52] Without such actions, the jury believed the player would not have died.

Since it was readily foreseeable that a club would again conduct hazing activities in violation of system rules, the court did not accept the defendants' argument that they had no specific knowledge of the actual hazing session.[53]

Conversely, certain defendant behavior may be judged as not the proximate cause of an injury.

- Inattention in preparing an athletic eligibility list led to a 20-year-old playing high school football.[54] No causal relationship was found to link such behavior to the plaintiff's death.
- A custodian violated board policy by letting high school students in to play basketball over Christmas vacation.[55] Lack of supervision, use of an old, slippery basketball, and a dirty playing floor were not found to be causally related to the injury that resulted when two players collided.

- Failure to provide a three-foot thick mat under gymnastics equipment was not found to be the proximate cause of an athlete's paralysis. The jury heard expert testimony that a mat of such thickness had not yet even been manufactured![56]

An Alaska case offers two intervening acts to supersede any wrongful defendant behavior.[57] Elementary school students were excused from school, with parental permission, to participate in an all-day AAU wrestling tournament. Parents were to provide transportation home, though the school transported the students to the tournament in the morning. Several boys requested one of the mothers to take them to lunch during a break in the matches. On the way, she stopped to get gas and asked her young son to refuel the car. In that process, gas overflowed onto her son's and the plaintiff's pants. She told the boys to get in the car and leave the gas alone as it would evaporate. While she went inside a shop, her son lit his own pants, extinguished the fire, and then lit the plaintiff's pants.

Even if the district had any legal duty to the plaintiff, the acts of the mother and her son were superseding intervening acts.

Under criminal law a fine for having committed an act is used as a punishment and bears no necessary relationship to any injury suffered by society. In tort law, the general belief is that an injured person should be made whole again; therefore, he should only receive damages equivalent to the actual loss. While some states allow so-called "punitive damages" (which appear to be analogous to fines in criminal law), these punitive damages do not exist unanimously across the country, nor are they generally favored by the courts.

Defenses to a Claim

In a general sense, the two best defenses to put forth are: one of the four elements is not proven; and governmental immunity bars the suit. If those are unavailable, however, so-called affirmative defenses may also be available. These are: contributory negligence, comparative negligence, and assumption of the risk.

The concept of contributory negligence suggests that, had the complaining party acted as a reasonably prudent person, he would not have placed himself in a situation which resulted in the injuries actually suffered. This is an objective standard as the behavior of the plaintiff is compared to that of the reasonable person. What the plaintiff thinks he is doing is not relevant. Would a reasonable person have behaved this way?

While anyone is capable of contributory negligence, courts have traditionally considered the age, physical characteristics, sex, and training of students in determining how a reasonably prudent plaintiff would have behaved under the circumstances. These considerations have lessened the likelihood that courts would find young children contributorily negligent.

The previously discussed case of the boys using the dilapidated truck illustrates a case of a jury judging a student by a non-adult standard and finding no contributory negligence.[58] A similar conclusion was reached in the case of the mentally handicapped student who ran out into the busy street.[59]

Remember that lack of "training" may be a factor in defeating a defense of contributory negligence where students are placed at unfamiliar tasks with unfamiliar equipment. Such was the case of the student injured by the malfunctioning fog machine.[60] Also, because a finding of contributory negligence traditionally allows recovery of *no* damages, courts have found it difficult to say that because a child "sort of" contributed to his own injury, while the educator contributed "significantly" to the injury, the child should have no recovery at all.

How is contributory negligence proven? The surrounding circumstances are a significant factor. For example, a 15-year-old student left a school program in progress in a darkened auditorium when a group became noisy and she knew no teachers were present. She was struck in the eye by a metal object. The court determined that in that situation, a reasonable person would not have left the auditorium, and, in fact, no other students left before the girl was struck in the eye.[61]

The 17-year-old who fell through the hatchway in the stage after the lights went out was judged negligent.[62] She not only ran around in complete darkness, but did not attempt to use the readily accessible, nearby exit.

Two drowning deaths during field trips provide more examples. A non-swimmer dove off the diving board, and another student attempted to swim out to a floating raft.[63] No evidence of clowning around or being pushed was present. In both instances the court determined the trips were well-planned and the accidents not attributable to any failings of the plaintiffs.

As another example, a senior basketball player ran through a glass panel three feet from the end of the baseline.[64] He was thoroughly familiar with the gymnasium and the location of the glass. He was running "wind sprints" at full speed, which he had done in each of the three previous years on the team. The fact that the coach had told the players to run at full speed did not reduce the plaintiff's own culpability.

Several states, either by statute or judicial decision, reacted to the harsh result of applying contributory negligence by developing a doctrine called comparative negligence. While the schemes differ from state to state, comparative negligence generally allows the jury to determine the relative percentages contributed to the injury by both the plaintiff and the defendant. For example, the jury might determine that the defendant-principal caused 75 percent of the injury, while the student was responsible for 25 percent of the injury. Thus, a $100,000 injury would result in award of $75,000 in damages by the defendant-principal to the plaintiff-student.

Similar to contributory negligence, assumption of the risk is a defense which requires a proof that the plaintiff *knowingly* and *voluntarily* accepted the dangers and risks involved in an activity.

While it is essential that the plaintiff legally assuming the risk has knowledge of the risks *actually* involved, this knowledge of risk is an even more significant factor when students are involved. The same factors that the courts consider in determining the ability of the student to be contributorily negligent are considered with the assumption of the risk. Specifically, the court would consider age, physical characteristics, sex, and training of the student involved. The general presumption exists also that participants in sporting events assume the normal risks associated with the sport. This is especially true when the athlete has had prior experience with the activity.[65]

Spectators have been found to have assumed the risk of injury when they stood along the sidelines of a football field.[66] The lack of alternative seating or crowd control did not affect the outcomes.

On the other hand, an athlete only assumes the *normal* risks of the game. The hockey player who was injured while wearing a defective helmet had not assumed the risk of faulty equipment, especially since he would not be expected to be an expert in equipment construction.[67] Further, a participant never assumes the risk that another person will be negligent. A wrestler was seriously injured while the referee turned away for 10 seconds to push the mats back together.[68] Had the same injury occurred while the referee was paying attention, the result might have been different.

Avoiding Claims of Negligence

Claims themselves cannot be completely avoided, but successful claims can be greatly reduced. Below are some suggestions for a principal.

1. Adopt a philosophy of paying attention to situations which could cause injury to students. Remember that the test often applied in a negligence case is whether the injury which occurred was foreseeable.
2. Adopt and constantly publicize system, school, departmental, and classroom rules. Do this to and for *students*. Do this to and for *staff*.
3. Document what was said when safety instructions are given, when it was said, to whom it was said, and what was done to assure understanding and compliance.
4. Conduct planned inspections both inside and outside buildings. In these days of "energy audits," the same attention should be given to "safety audits."
5. Post *understandable* warning signs in potentially dangerous locations. Use signs appropriate for the age, training, and maturity of the people affected.
6. If an activity appears to involve inherent risk of injury, try to reduce that risk or consider an alternate activity.
7. Be certain that students can perform what is required in order to prevent injuries. Special care must be given to people with mental or physical handicaps.
8. Take extra precautions for away-from-campus activities. Ability to control such activities is very often much less than with in-school activities. The greater the risk of injury inherent in the activitiy (e.g., going to the beach), the greater are the plans required. Relate quantity of supervision to the age and training of the participants. While permission slips do *not* automatically relieve educators of legal liability, they do provide evidence of the quality of planning and of knowledge and consent by parents which may be valuable in

defending against claims should injury occur. Also, find out whether volunteer drivers are covered by the system's insurance policy.

9. Secure liability insurance. Either be certain that the system provides such protection or purchase coverage for yourself. State professional education groups offer insurance at relatively inexpensive group rates and it is offered as an automatic benefit of NASSP membership.[69] Be certain to read the fine print of all policies to be sure of the nature and amounts of coverage.

Summary

Liability for personal injuries can be faced by all educators, from board members, to teachers, to custodians. In our litigious society every school person can best avoid a successful tort suit by behaving as the "reasonable person" would.

Negligence, or accidental injury, is the most common tort in the school setting. The law has created numerous barriers which make it difficult for a plaintiff to establish a negligence claim. Generally speaking, avoiding injuries by "being on the lookout" for dangerous situations and taking appropriate precautions ahead of time is the best defense against such claims, as well as protecting the students in your charge.

Footnotes

1. Macomb v. Gould, 244 N.E.2d 634 (Ill. App. 1969).
2. Hogenson v. Williams, 542 S.W.2d 456 (Tex. Civ. App. 1976).
3. Biddle v. Mazzacco, 324 P.2d 364, 366 (Alaska 1955).
4. A. P. Herbert, Misleading Cases in Common Law, 12-16 (1930).
5. Lehmuth v. Long Beach Unified Sch. Dist., 348 P.2d 887, 890 (Calif. 1960).
6. Palsgraf v. Long Island R.R. Co., 162 N.E. 99 (Ct. of App. of N.Y. 1928).
7. See e.g., Turner v. Caddo Parish School Board, 214 So. 2d 153 (La. 1968).
8. Cox v. Barnes et al., 464 S.W. 2d 61 (Ky. Ct. of App. 1971).
9. Montag v. Board of Education, 446 N.E.2d 299 (Ill. App. 1983); O'Brien v. Township High Sch. Dist., 415 N.E.2d 1015 (Ill. 1980); Lynch v. Board of Educ., 412 N.E.2d 447 (Ill. 1980); Borushek v. Kincaid, 397 N.E.2d 172 (Ill. App. 1979); Thomas v. Chicago Bd. of Educ., 395 N.E.2d 538 (Ill. 1979); Friederich v. Board of Educ., 375 N.E.2d 141 (Ill. App. 1978); Gerrity v. Beatty, 373 N.E.2d 1323 (Ill. 1978); Tanari v. School Directors, 373 N.E.2d 5 (Ill. 1977); Kobylanski v. Chicago Bd. of Educ., 347 N.E.2d 705 (Ill. 1976).
10. Sims v. Etowah County Bd. of Educ., 337 So.2d 1310 (Ala. 1976); Churilla v. School Dist., 306 N.W.2d 381 (Mich. App. 1981); Castro v. Los Angeles Bd. of Educ., 126 Cal. Rptr. 537 (Calif. App. 1976); Lovitt v. Concord Sch. Dist., 228 N.W.2d 479 (Mich. App. 1975); Morris v. Union High Sch. Dist., 294 P. 998 (Wash. 1931); Grames v. King, 332 N.W.2d 615 (Mich. App. 1983); Rupp v. Bryant, 417 So.2d 658 (Fla. 1982).
11. Stehn v. Bernarr MacFadden Founds., 434 F.2d 811 (6th Cir. 1970); Thomas v. St. Mary's Roman Catholic Church, 283 N.W.2d 254 (S.Dak. 1979).
12. Vargo v. Svitchan, 301 N.W.2d 1 (Mich. App. 1981).
13. Thomas v. Chicago Bd. of Educ., 395 N.E.2d 538 (Ill. 1979).
14. Byrns v. Riddell, Inc., 550 P.2d 1065 (Ariz. 1976).
15. Stehn v. Bernarr MacFadden Founds., 434 F.2d 811 (6th Cir. 1970); Carabba v. Anacortes Sch. Dist., 435 P.2d 936 (Wash. 1968); Chappel v. Franklin Pierce Sch. Dist., 426 P.2d 471 (Wash. 1967); Rupp v. Bryant, 417 So.2d 658 (Fla. 1982); Tanari v. School Directors, 373 N.E.2d 5 (Ill. 1977).
16. Borushek v. Kincaid, 397 N.E.2d 172 (Ill. App. 1979); Tanari v. School Directors, 373 N.E.2d 5 (Ill. 1977).

17. Foster v. Houston Gen. Ins. Co., 407 So.2d 759 (La. App. 1981).
18. Rupp v. Bryant, 417 So.2d 658 (Fla. 1982); DeGooyer v. Harkness, 13 N.W.2d 815 (S.Dak. 1944).
19. Thomas v. St. Mary's Roman Catholic Church, 283 N.W.2d 254 (S.Dak. 1979).
20. Morris v. Douglas County Sch. Dist., 403 P.2d 775 (Oreg. 1965).
21. Rawls v. Dugas, 398 So.2d 630 (La. App. 1981).
22. Akins v. Glens Falls City Sch. Dist., 441 N.Y.S.2d 644 (N.Y. 1981).
23. Perry v. Seattle Sch. Dist., 405 P.2d 589 (Wash. 1965).
24. Plesnicar v. Kovach, 430 N.E.2d 648 (Ill. App. 1981).
25. Friederich v. Board of Educ., 375 N.E.2d 141 (Ill. App. 1978).
26. Jackson v. Cartwright Sch. Dist., 607 P.2d 975 (Ariz. App. 1980).
27. Hunt v. Scotia-Glenville Central Sch. Dist., 460 N.Y.S.2d 205 (App. Div. 1983).
28. Mancha v. Field Museum of Natural History, 283 N.E.2d 899 (Ill. App. 1972).
29. Lynch v. Board of Educ., 412 N.E.2d 447 (Ill. 1980); Woodman v. Hemet Union High Sch. Dist., 29 P.2d 257 (Calif. App. 1934).
30. Weldy v. Oakland High Sch. Dist., 65 P.2d 851 (Calif. App. 1937).
31. Mogabab v. Orleans Parish Sch. Bd., 239 So.2d 456 (La. App. 1970).
32. Thomas v. St. Mary's Roman Catholic Church, 283 N.W.2d 254 (S.Dak. 1979).
33. Woodman v. Hemet Union High Sch. Dist., 29 P.2d 257 (Calif. App. 1934).
34. DeGooyer v. Harkness, 13 N.W.2d 815 (S.Dak. 1944).
35. Lynch v. Board of Educ., 412 N.E.2d 447 (Ill. 1980).
36. Everett v. Bucky Warren, Inc., 380 N.E.2d 653 (Mass. 1978).
37. Morris v. Douglas County Sch. Dist., 403 P.2d 775 (Oreg. 1965).
38. Williamson v. Board of Educ., 375 N.Y.S.2d 221 (App. Div. 1975).
39. Raleigh v. Independent Sch. Dist., 275 N.W.2d 572 (Minn. 1978).
40. Foster v. Houston Gen. Ins. Co., 407 So.2d 759 (La. 1981).
41. Wesley v. Page, 514 S.W.2d 697 (Ky. App. 1974).
42. Tanari v. School Directors, 373 N.E.2d 5 (Ill. 1977).
43. Vargo v. Svitchan, 301 N.W.2d 1 (Mich. App. 1981).
44. Borushek v. Kincaid, 397 N.E.2d 172 (Ill. App. 1979); Nunez v. Isidore Neuman High Sch., 306 So.2d 457 (La. App. 1975).
45. Vendrell v. School Dist., 376 P.2d 406 (Oreg. 1962).
46. Tannenbaum v. Board of Educ., 255 N.Y.S.2d 522 (App. Div. 1964), *aff'd.*, 214 N.E.2d 378 (N.Y. 1966).
47. Black's Law Dictionary 1391 (4th ed. 1968).
48. Meyer v. Board of Educ., 86 A.2d 761, 765 (N.J. 1952).
49. Raleigh v. Independent Sch. Dist., 275 N.W.2d 573 (Minn. 1978).
50. Potter v. North Carolina Sch. of the Arts, 245 S.E.2d 188 (N.C. App. 1978).
51. DeGooyer v. Harkness, 13 N.W.2d 815 (S.Dak. 1944).
52. Mogabab v. Orleans Parish Sch. Bd., 239 So.2d 456 (La. App. 1970).
53. Rupp v. Bryant, 417 So.2d 658 (Fla. 1982).
54. Barrett v. Phillips, 223 S.E.2d 918 (N.C. App. 1976).
55. Albers v. Independent Sch. Dist., 487 P.2d 936 (Idaho 1971).
56. Montag v. Board of Educ., 446 N.E.2d 299 (Ill. App. 1983).
57. Sharp v. Fairbanks North Star Borough, 569 P.2d 178 (Alaska Div. 1964).
58. Woodman v. Hemet Union High Sch. Dist., 29 P.2d 257 (Calif. App. 1934).
59. Foster v. Houston Gen. Ins. Co., 407 So.2d 759 (La. App. 1981).
60. Potter v. North Carolina Sch. of the Arts, 245 S.E.2d 188 (N.C. App. 1978).
61. Viveiros v. Hawaii, 513 P.2d 487 (Hawaii 1973).
62. Tannenbaum v. Board of Educ., 255 N.Y.S.2d 522 (App. Div. 1964), *aff'd.* 214 N.E.2d 378 (N.Y. 1966).
63. Powell v. Orleans Parish Sch. Bd., 354 So.2d 229 (La. Ct. of App. 1978); Cox v. Barnes, 469 S.W.2d 61 (Ky. App. 1971).
64. Clary v. Alexander County Bd. of Educ., 199 S.E.2d 738 (N.C. App. 1973).
65. Albers v. Independent Sch. Dist., 487 P.2d 936 (Idaho 1971); Vendrell v. Sch. Dist., 376 P.2d 406 (Oreg. 1962); Rutter v. Northeastern Beaver County Sch. Dist., 423 A.2d 1035 (Pa. Super. 1980); Passantino v. Board of Educ., 363 N.E.2d 1373 (N.Y. 1977).
66. Perry v. Seattle Sch. Dist., 405 P.2d 589 (Wash. 1965); Cadieux v. Board of Educ., 266 N.Y.S.2d 895 (App. Div. 1966).
67. Everett v. Bucky Warren, Inc., 380 N.E.2d 653 (Mass. 1978).
68. Carabba v. Anacortes Sch. Dist., 435 P.2d 936 (Wash. 1967).
69. Goldberg, *Liability Insurance for High School Athletes Endorsed in 47 States,* Education Week, at 5, col. 1.

Chapter IV

Coaches and Sponsors

Two aspects of law affecting student activities personnel are assignment and removal. Research has revealed few cases specifically related to student activities' personnel and the law, but a brief review of the law governing teacher personnel may be of value. A general course or book on educational personnel and the law would provide much greater depth than is possible here, and the impact of state statutes, board policies, collective bargaining agreements, and individual teacher contracts must be identified by the reader to assure he or she has complete access to relevant law.

Assignment

The handful of court cases that have challenged the assignment authority of public school officials almost always cited the *Parrish* and *McGrath* cases.[1] Both cases expressed the view that school boards and administrators possess broad authority to assign teachers to service outside the regular academic setting.

The courts agreed that teachers are not hourly employees and that their duties inherently include school responsibilities other than teaching subject matter; thus, boards need not pay additional compensation for such assignments. Further, such assignments may occur outside the regular school day. This authority rests impliedly with school officials, if not expressly stated in state law.[2]

Building on this basic principle, the *Parrish* and *McGrath* courts identified some activities to which teachers may reasonably be assigned. These include: supervising students' meetings; coaching plays; coaching intramural and interscholastic athletic teams; supervising field trips; and supervising students at athletic contests and social events.

That these activities might occur on Saturdays, in the evenings, or during school holidays, did not diminish the board's assignment authority. In fact, an Illinois court refused to apply a state statute forbidding teaching on Saturday and holidays by concluding that the statute was not intended to apply to non-academic school activities.[3] Thus, teachers could legally be assigned supervising, but not teaching duties, at those times! Courts have approved the selection of a prospective teacher based on fitness and enthusiasm for sponsoring cocurricular activities.[4]

Is this assignment authority at all limited? Again, *Parrish* and *McGrath* recognized that certain tasks could be *outside* a reasonable concept of teaching duties. Therefore, assignment to perform janitorial tasks, police duties, or school bus driving would not be within that vast discretion. Additionally, such assignments should be reasonable in number and hours of duty and equally distributed among the staff.[5] Courts also have determined that assignments should be related to a teacher's interest and expertise.[6]

Can refusal to carry out such assignments cause a teacher legal difficulties? Yes. For example, an untenured teacher was not rehired because he continued to refuse to perform cocurricular activity duties.[7] Even though no specific refusals were mentioned, except for a refusal to assist in an identification photo project, the court accepted the principal's generalized accusation to support the teacher's non-renewal.

When most of the coaches and sponsors of school activities in a school system resigned from such assignments *en masse,* the school board went to court seeking an injunction and characterizing the action as an illegal strike. The court agreed that such assignments were within the authority of the board, that the action was a strike, and proceeded to issue the injunction.[8]

Principals should keep this vast authority over assignment in mind. The greatest personnel problem facing principals today may be the coach/sponsor who, after a few years, declines to continue. Convincing the person to accept a building transfer or overstaffing a building is the usual solution. Trying to terminate the individual on the grounds of "justifiable decrease in the number of teaching positions" or "other good and just cause" have been tried without great success.

Could legally-sound arguments for "insubordination" or "neglect of duty" be raised? No cases were found where these arguments were made, but with the vast power to assign sponsors and coaches, any refusal might prove legally detrimental to the teacher.

Does a school board ever lose on a challenge? While expressing his willingness to accept assignment to another cocurricular activity, George Pease refused to sponsor a boys' bowling club. The activity was held once a week for two-and-a-half hours after school. Though it was sanctioned by the school, no expenses were borne by the district, and it was not part of any interscholastic or intramural program.

In due course, the board terminated Pease for incompetence, persistent negligence, and willful violation of school rules. Despite his completely satisfactory ratings as a classroom teacher, refusal to accept this assignment led to his termination.

While supporting the general logic of *Parrish* and *McGrath,* the Supreme Court of Pennsylvania determined this assignment was not so related to the school program as to come within board authority to make supervisory assignments. Pease was ordered reinstated.[9]

With the advent of collective bargaining, the question of cocurricular activity assignments has become a matter of negotiation. One court determined that the decisions to have any cocurricular activities and identification of those activities were matters of educational policy purely for the school board's judgment. However, the court did determine that the assignment process and compensation were subjects for negotiation.[10]

A new challenge to the authority of school officials arose in the courts in the late 1970s. Questions of equal pay and discrimination based on sex were raised by female coaches. Federal statutes such as Title VI, Title VII, Title IX, the Equal Pay Act, and §1983 prohibiting discrimination based on race, age, religion, and sex, were used to establish federal judicial claims of discrimination.[11] Proof of such claims could bring the plaintiffs not only back pay and appointment to the desired positions, but could cause the defendant school system and officials to pay monetary damage awards and attorney fees, and lose federal funds. Several states adopted similar, and in some instances, more far-reaching statutes to prevent discrimination.

Though the law relating to this subject is very new and very unsettled, some guidance can be given. Discussion will focus on several claims of sex discrimination.

Where different levels of duties for the girls' basketball coach and the boys' basketball coach can be identified, a board can be justified in having different levels of pay.[12] In one interesting example of this principle, a coach had diligently worked to upgrade the program for girls' tennis. By so doing, she had raised her duties to a level comparable to that of the boys' tennis coach. Because the coach *herself* had extended the requirements of her coaching position without board authorization, the court ruled that the system had no obligation to provide equal pay under Pennsylvania's sex discrimination laws.[13]

While nothing can substitute for expertise to ensure compliance with the whole array of federal and state anti-discrimination statutes, one case particularly demonstrates what the principal should *not* do.[14]

In the early 1970s, Moundsville Junior High School in Marshall County, W.Va., had no interscholastic girls' basketball team. The plaintiff, Linda Burkey, organized a girls' basketball team, and during a four-year-period, the team won 31 games, lost 4, forfeited 1, and had a championship team in 1975. Burkey received numerous letters of commendation from her supervising principals.

For the first three years, she received no compensation for coaching and, during the last year, she was paid half of the salary the boys' coaches received. Male coaches of girls' junior high sports received the same compensation that Linda Burkey received. From 1973 to '78, the plaintiff tried various state and federal administrative remedies to resolve her claim of sex discrimination, but to no avail.

In March of 1976, Burkey was transferred from her junior high school teaching position to an elementary school and was removed as coach of the junior high school basketball team. Simultaneously, a second coaching position for girls' basketball at Moundsville Junior High School was created. In federal court, Burkey brought claims under Title VII, §1983, and the Equal Pay Act. She claimed that she had been denied equal pay, had not been given the opportunity to coach boys' sports, had been transferred from her teaching position, had been removed from her coaching position in retaliation for her claims of sex discrimination, and had been denied a later request for reassignment to teaching and coaching positions at the local high school. The court found for the plaintiff on all of her complaints and ordered that she receive back pay, be offered the next teaching position for girls' basketball at such school, and be paid interest on back pay and attorney fees for the years of litigation.

When considering the full impact of such discrimination cases, one should remember the possibility of damages under *Wood v. Strickland* coming *personally* from board members and administrators who perpetuate such discrimination.

Transfer or Removal

In 1969, the Supreme Court reminded public school officials that neither teachers nor students shed their constitutional rights at the schoolhouse gate.[15] Although such rights are never absolute, coaches and sponsors retain such rights as freedom of speech. As a general statement of law, a public school employee may not be terminated, transferred, demoted, or reduced in pay for exercising constitutional rights.

Late in the school year, after Raymond Jergeson had already signed a contract for the coming year, he received notice from the board that he would be dismissed.[16] In addition to a general charge of incompetency based on the April Fool's edition of the school newspaper (of which he was the adviser), there was also a broader statement reflecting board disagreement with the teacher's philosophy and practice of education. Several instances were cited to support the charges: failing to censor the school newspaper; approving a picture of a row of urinals; permitting articles in the newspaper critical of the disciplinary actions of certain teachers; including complaints about the administration and board; allowing a dirty poem to remain on the blackboard in his classroom for two weeks; presenting a personal appearance that did not set a good example for high school students; and several miscellaneous incidents reflecting on his teaching style.

In agreeing with the decision of the board to terminate Jergeson, the Supreme Court of Wyoming appeared to be convinced by the quantity of charges and incidents. The court apparently accepted the proposition that the school newspaper adviser could be expected to censor the contents of the newspaper. Cases earlier in this monograph which discuss the First Amendment rights of students as they relate to publications suggest the possible impropriety of such an expectation for the adviser. Perhaps the Wyoming court did not make a great effort to determine exactly which of the charges and incidents were legally usable and which were not, but the court concluded that enough existed overall to support the board's judgment.

In Little Rock, Arkansas, a public school teacher was terminated for offering her students higher grades if they purchased raffle tickets from her. The opinion does not indicate whether the tickets were for a school-related raffle, but none of the tickets were actually sold. A board finding of unprofessional conduct was upheld by the appellate court.[17]

A teacher-football coach who continually disagreed with his principal was ultimately removed at the end of the season.[18] During the height of the controversy—from June to the end of November—several confrontations took place.

The coach, Shimoyama, wrote a strongly-worded letter questioning the accuracy of the administration's complaints, attacking the principal personally, emphasizing the coach's contribution to the football program at the school, and personally rebuking the principal. Apparently, the letter was shared with the school booster club, the assistant football coach, and representatives of the teachers' union. Prior to the start of the 1978 football season, the principal and coach agreed that he would coach through the season and that a reevaluation would be conducted at the end of the season.

Upon reevaluation, the principal determined that the coach should be removed from further coaching duties. Shimoyama claimed that his free speech rights were violated. He argued specifically that his verbal and written statements to the principal were protected by the First Amendment; therefore, they could not be used as grounds for termination.

A California state appellate court concluded that personal attacks upon an immediate superior, because of the negative impact on the working relationship, were not protected, and whether the letter had entered into the principal's decision did not legally matter because of the presence of sufficient documentation of several instances to justify the removal.

In a similar vein, a Texas coach who criticized the school's athletic program and requested new basketballs and warm-up suits, claimed denial of free speech, due process, and equal protection when he was terminated during the school year.[19] The Court of Appeals for the Fifth Circuit upheld a district court determination that repeated threats on the lives of superiors and colleagues, rather than exercise of constitutional rights, provided proper grounds for termination.

While these four cases may have had expected outcomes, school boards can lose seemingly similar cases. An Alabama coach noticed that gate receipts for home football games were not as high as the number of people in the stands suggested.[20] After discussing his concern with the athletic booster club, a procedure was established for counting attendance to better judge gate receipts.

The principal, in charge of gate receipts, recommended that coach Abston not only be removed as coach, but that he not be renewed as a teacher within the system. (Abston had not yet attained tenure.) The superintendent and school board accepted the recommendations, notified the teacher that his contract would not be renewed, and subsequently accepted the resignation of the principal.

Because he was not tenured, Abston had no legal right to statutory due process of law to allow him to challenge the nonrenewal. However, Abston convinced the court that his exercise of free speech in questioning the gate receipts was a substantial factor in the decision not to rehire him. Applicable federal constitutional law indicated that when the plaintiff had succeeded in this showing, the burden then shifted to the school board to prove that it would not have renewed Abston even without considering the exercise of protected rights.

Because the trial court had not properly applied this principle, the Alabama Supreme Court remanded the case to the trial court to allow the board to present evidence justifying its decision. Given the Alabama Supreme Court's recitation of the facts in this case, the board could not likely justify its decision.

Jerry Anderson was removed from his coaching duties three weeks after he sent a letter directly to school board members.[21] The letter, characterized by the trial court as not critical of the district or the superintendent, contained Anderson's suggestions relating to athletic programs and policies in the district. The removal was based on a violation of the system's "channels" policy which required all communications to the board to go through the superintendent. Numerous pretrial motions were all decided substantially in favor of the coach. The judge found the particular letter to be within the scope of protected speech and found the channels policy to be an unconstitutional restraint on freedom of speech.

How can *Abston* and *Anderson* come out in favor of the plaintiff, as they apparently will, while *Jergeson, Shimoyama,* and *White* end as they do? One basic fact stands out in all three cases won by the board of education: the board appeared to have a large quantity and variety of credible evidence. While some elements of the charges were of questionable legal validity, enough other evidence appears to justify the result.

However, in *Abston* and *Anderson,* a general lack of any other logical basis for not renewing the coach was present other than that which was legally invalid. Additionally, while Shimoyama's criticisms were personal, as were Abston's, his complaints were aimed more at judgments and decisions of the principal rather than at the honesty of his use of public funds.

Controversy over the use of vulgar language and drinking scenes during a school drama production and rehearsal led to a board decision not to rehire a teacher who was also the dramatics director.[22] The board and superintendent claimed that Webb failed to abide by a rule forbidding vulgar language and drinking scenes in public productions.

The court determined that the removal was due to the teacher's exercise of academic freedom—the right to use teaching methods she judged to be reasonably appropriate for the task. More importantly, however, the court determined that the existence of any prohibition on vulgar language and drinking scenes was questionable. Even if the rule did exist, its precise meaning was not accurately explained to the teacher; hence, her removal violated a basic rule of due process, that a person not be punished for a rule about which she did not have fair notice.

Finally, the court concluded that the board could validly adopt such prohibitions in policy so long as it assured accurate and comprehensive notification to the parties affected.

A 1982 Nebraska case raised an interesting question.[23] Can one's sponsorship of student activities be used as a factor in a reduction-in-force policy? The local school board adopted a reduction-in-force policy pursuant to a Nebraska statute. In determining how to reduce tenured teachers, the board listed five factors in order of priority. The first three factors were:

1. Certification and area(s) of endorsement
2. Program to be offered
3. Contribution to the activity program.

The system determined that it was necessary to eliminate one business education teaching position. The two business ed teachers were equal on the first two priority items. On priority three (contribution to the activity program) one teacher, who was subsequently terminated, was cosponsor of the yearbook and sponsor of the sophomore class. The teacher who was retained was the assistant volleyball coach, head girls' basketball coach, and cosponsor of the school lettermen's club. The Nebraska Supreme Cour concluded that the board had wide discretion to make these judgments, and the particular policy and decision challenged were not arbitrary and capricious. It ruled in favor of the board.

The final case about substantive rights considers the scope of authority of the state activities association in the employment of school personnel.[24] The Arkansas Activity Association found that a member high school had conducted out-of-season football practices in violation of association rules. The school was notified that it had two choices: Either the school could fire the coach and be placed on probation for one year, or the school would be suspended from fielding a football team for one year.

The coach had already signed a contract both as teacher and coach for that football season. The rule prohibiting off-season football practices did not include a warning that a coach's contract of employment could be affected if the rule were broken. Because of this, the court found the association's efforts to be invalid.

Based on this opinion, such a rule with a penalty appropriately included apparently could be promulgated by the association. If that were indeed the message, the two-party employment relationship between the school board and coach could be seriously affected. Perhaps administrators should consider placing in the contracts of coaches and sponsors, a statement to the effect that rules of athletic and activity associations are incorporated into the provisions of the employment contract.

In several cases, coaches who were relieved of coaching duties sought the due process protections of their state tenure laws. Courts have generally found that tenure laws do not apply to the termination of a person's coaching responsibilities.[25] Rather, any protection the teacher-coach might have comes only from the coaching contract.

An Illinois coach was awarded $20,000 when he was terminated without any reasons or hearing prior to the second year of a two-year contract.[26] The board argued that state law limited all contracts to one year, but the court determined the board had verbally committed itself to a two-year contract.

The Tennessee Supreme Court made a slightly different interpretation, finding that while the termination portions of the Tenure Act did not apply, the transfer provisions applied.[27] However, the coach was unsuccessful in his challenge because the school board had complied with the transfer requirements.

When the Alabama Supreme Court determined that transfer provisions for a tenured teacher applied to the transfer from head football coach to head basketball coach, the implications were greater.[28] In Alabama, the process required for transfer of a tenured teacher is slightly more complicated than in Tennessee, and thus, it would be hard to transfer a coach who also was a tenured teacher.

Interestingly, the court ruled for the school board because the coach had challenged the transfer as a termination and had followed the procedures required under the termination provisions of Alabama law rather than following the transfer provisions. The interpretation and application of the transfer provisions of Alabama statutes may be the broadest in the country and may not be a good example of typical law throughout the United States.

What if a principal wants to remove a coach (who is a tenured teacher) from both the coaching position and the teaching position? Could incompetence *as a coach* or neglect of duty *as a coach* be documented and used as grounds for termination?

A recent Iowa case offers interesting insight into this issue.[29] Larry Munger was a social studies teacher, assistant football coach, and head wrestling coach. Under the ''just cause'' ground in the tenured teacher statutes, Munger was terminated for failure to: maintain a competitive program; show signs of becoming competitive; maintain rapport with athletes; and convince athletes of the importance of the program. No complaints about his teaching or football coaching were made.

Even though Munger offered to resign as wrestling coach, the board terminated him. The Supreme Court of Iowa determined the board did not have enough evidence to substantiate the charges.

What is important is how the court handled the whole idea of terminating a teacher for incompetency as a coach in one sport. The court said that while some contracts are severable, his contract was not divisible. To allow him to pick and choose his duties would not be feasible. Thus, the concept of termination based on one's failings as a coach or sponsor, though not supported by the evidence in this particular case, was recognized.

The admonition in the discussion of assigning coaches and sponsors to consider claims for discrimination based on race, sex, age, or religion is equally applicable here. A black assistant football coach was removed because the board wanted the new head coach to have some flexibility in structuring his program. The racial discrimination claim was defeated by evidence showing the plaintiff was replaced with a black as well as by testimony demonstrating practical, non-discriminatory reasons for the change.[30]

In the process of removing a coach (or a teacher for that matter), principals should guard against public statements which could damage a person's constitutional liberty right in his professional and personal reputation. Consideration should be given to whether public statements might impose a "stigma" on a person such that future employment opportunities or community standing might be seriously harmed.[31]

Summary

Considering the large number of schools, personnel, and student activities, very few reported cases have involved such personnel matters. Statistically, that would suggest an unlikelihood that any school system would ever be taken to court over student activity programs. However, this litigation-conscious society, with its proliferating laws and regulations, presents a continuing threat to the once-total rule of the principal and school board.

Before exercising discretion over assignment, transfer, and removal of coaches and sponsors, all relevant statutes and regulations, board policies, collective bargaining agreements, and teacher contracts must be studied to recognize the outer bounds on that discretion.

Footnotes

1. Parrish v. Moss, 106 N.Y.S.2d 557 (Sp. Term 1951); McGrath v. Burkhard, 280 P.2d 865 (Calif. App. 1955).
2. McGrath v. Burkhard, 280 P.2d 865 (Calif. App. 1955).
3. District 300 Educ. Ass'n. v. Board of Educ., 334 N.E.2d 165 (Ill. App. 1975).
4. Higgins v. Board of Educ., 286 S.E.2d 682 (W.Va. 1982).
5. Board of Educ. v. Asbury Park Educ. Ass'n., 368 A.2d 396 (N.J. Super. Ct. 1976); Hawkins v. Tyler City Bd. of Educ., 275 S.E.2d 908 (W.Va. 1981).
6. Board of Educ. v. Asbury Park Educ. Ass'n., 368 A.2d 396 (N.J. Super. Ct. 1976).
7. Simcox v. Board of Educ., 443 F.2d 40 (7th Cir. 1971). *Accord* Jackson v. Hazlehurst Mun. Separate Sch. Dist., 427 So.2d 134 (Miss. 1983).
8. Board of Educ. v. Asbury Park Educ. Ass'n., 368 A.2d 396 (N.J. Super. Ct. 1976).
9. Pease v. Millcreek Township Sch. Dist., 195 A.2d 104 (Pa. 1963).
10. West Hartford Educ. Ass'n. v. De Courcy, 295 A.2d 526 (Conn. 1972).
11. Strong v. Demopolis City Bd. of Educ., 515 F. Supp. 730 (S.D. Ala. 1981); Pegues v. Morehouse Parish Sch. Bd., 706 F.2d 735 (5th Cir. 1983).
12. State Division of Human Rights v. Syracuse City Teachers Ass'n., 412 N.Y.S.2d 711 (App. Div. 1979).
13. School Dist. v. Commonwealth Human Relations Comm'n., 368 A.2d 901 (Commw. Ct. 1977).
14. Burkey v. Marshall County Bd. of Educ., 513 F. Supp. 1084 (N.D. W.Va. 1981).
15. Tinker v. Des Moines Indep. Community Sch. Dist., 393 U.S. 503 (1969).
16. Jergeson v. Board of Trustees, 476 P.2d 481 (Wyo. 1970). *Accord* Nicholson v. Board of Educ., 682 F.2d 858 (9th Cir. 1982).
17. Gatewood v. Little Rock Pub. Schools, 616 S.W.2d 784 (Ark. App. 1981).
18. Shimoyama v. Board of Educ., 174 Calif. Rptr. 749 (Calif. App. 1981).
19. White v. South Park Indep. Sch. Dist., 693 F.2d 1163 (5th Cir. 1982).
20. Abston v. Woodard, So.2d 237 (Ala. 1981).
21. Anderson v. Central Point Sch. Dist., 554 F. Supp. 600 (D. Oreg. 1982).
22. Webb v. Lake Mills Community Sch. Dist., 344 F. Supp. 791 (N.D. Iowa 1972).
23. Dykeman v. Board of Educ., 316 N.W.2d 69 (Nebr. 1982).
24. Wright v. Arkansas Act. Ass'n., 501 F.2d 25 (8th Cir. 1974).
25. Neal v. School Dist., 205 Neb. 558 (1980); Goodwin v. Bennett County High Sch. Indep. Sch. Dist., 226 N.W.2d 166 (S.Dak. 1975); Smith v. Board of Educ., 708 F.2d 258 (7th Cir. 1983).
26. Vail v. Board of Educ., 706 F.2d 1435 (7th Cir. 1983).
27. White v. Banks, 614 S.W.2d 331 (Tenn. 1981).
28. Greene v. County Bd. of Educ., 197 So.2d 771 (Ala. 1967).
29. Munger v. Jesup Community Sch. Dist., 325 N.W.2d 377 (Iowa 1982). See *e.g.*, Board of Educ. v. Youel, 282 N.W.2d 677 (Iowa 1979); Smith v. Board of Educ., 708 F.2d 258 (7th Cir. 1983).
30. Lee v. Ozark City Bd. of Educ., 517 F. Supp. 686 (M.D. Ala. 1981).
31. Smith v. Board of Educ., 708 F.2d 258 (7th Cir. 1983).

Chapter V

School Money and Property

Very few reported cases involve the use of school money and property for student activities. The two initial questions to be considered are: Whose money is it? and Who controls the money?

A Pennsylvania school board operated on the theory that athletic activities, high school band organizations, and other student activities were completely separate from those which require board control. The board delegated complete decision-making authority and control of money to an athletic control board and did not oversee the activities of that body. One implication of such delegation was that the state competitive bid law was avoided. The court concluded that all receipts and all expenditures must be approved by the board of education as part of its legal mandate from the state.[1] An athletic control board could continue in an advisory capacity, but decisions must be made by the board.

Another Pennsylvania case involved school activities' checking and savings accounts put under the sole control of the principal.[2] The board of education claimed it was not in charge of the funds, therefore, the funds were not subject to statutory auditing requirements. The board indicated that two of its members did conduct an informal audit of the accounts yearly. Additionally, some tax funds were intermingled in these student activity accounts.

Once again, the court concluded that these were school funds and were subject to state auditing laws, regardless of whether tax revenues were intermingled with the activities funds. The court stated that "where monies or property are derived directly or indirectly through the use of school buildings, or from the expenditures of public funds of the district, these revenues are public property, and must be handled exactly as tax monies and be paid to the district treasurer."[3]

A Kentucky court arrived at a similar definition of school funds based on a completely different set of facts.[4] A state law forbade board members from direct or indirect interest in sales to the board of which they were members. In this case a board member was a co-owner of a soft drink company which supplied its product to schools in the county. Profits from the student sales went to the student activity fund.

Concluding that activity funds were school funds for purposes of the statutes, the court determined that the board member had violated the statute and had vacated his office.

Not only can board members face a problem, as the Kentucky board member found, but administrators can face ethical and legal questions about accounting for activity funds. A Mississippi board of education went to court to demand an accounting of school funds by one of its principals.[5] No existing statutes regulated the handling of these accounts. The principal had been taking revenue from one source and spending it for unrelated activities. Because the evidence was contradictory, the court could not conclude that the school board had demonstrated misuse of funds, and thus ruled for the principal.

However, in the absence of the state law, the court offered suggested procedures for administrators to follow:

> It appears to this Court that one who is authorized to receive "activities funds" should make, as a minimum, at least some record of how much he receives, from whom, and for what purpose he receives it, to whom he paid the funds, and on what account. When a school principal buys books, class rings, class annuals, class pictures and other articles, and equipment for resale to the students—or on order from the students—the sums paid by the students should be applied to that particular account payable and should not be applied to other school activities.[6]

Another legal issue concerns fees for school in general, and for certain student activities in particular. As will be illustrated in the following three cases, reference to state law and state court opinions is essential in identifying the legal status of such fees for student activities in any given state.

The Idaho Supreme Court ruled that activity fees could not be assessed on all students;[7] however, those students who actually participate in a specific activity could be charged a fee because these were offerings outside the regular curriculum of schools as contemplated by the constitution.

The Montana state constitution contained a similar requirement for "free, common schools." Could a school system charge for athletic equipment, towel usage, insurance for interscholastic sports, yearbooks, pictures, and so on? While avoiding a decision on each of the specific fees, the court expressed the principle that fees for a course or activity "reasonably related to recognized academic and educational goals of the particular school system" could not be levied.[8]

Although this statement could be interpreted to preclude fees for student activities, other language in the opinion suggests that relationship to graduation requirements may determine which courses could have fees.

Finally, the Supreme Court of North Carolina interpreted a state constitutional provision requiring "free public schools" to mean "free" only in the sense of "free from tuition."[9] The court upheld the levying of innumerable charges for curricular and cocurricular activities that were being charged by almost all school systems in the state.

In states where fees are commonplace, students from poor families may not be able to share in the whole array of educational activities. Several Illinois students whose families received Aid to Families with Dependent Children sued to force either the public schools or the state department of public aid to pay the fees for these students. The fees were for such activities as graduation, dinner dance, graduation announcements, yearbook, class gift, class ribbon, and cap and gown. The federal district court, concluding that no constitutional rights and no unconstitutional denial of equal protection of the laws were involved, refused to grant the plaintiffs' request.[10]

Not only can the definition of cocurricular activities affect the school's ability to collect fees from students, but an Illinois case demonstrates how such definition affected the ability of the school system to secure reimbursement for transportation expenditures from the state.[11]

State auditors determined that a local school board should repay some $44,000 to the state for claimed expenses arising from late afternoon bus routes. The school system ran regular bus routes after school and then ran additional bus routes later in the afternoon for students who had remained for conferences with teachers, disciplinary punishment, sports programs, and club activities. Since the students had primarily come to school for typical school-day activities, providing late afternoon transportation was the obvious completion of the obligation to return students home from school.

When schools operate an ambitious student activity program, local merchants undoubtedly feel competition for the entertainment dollar. The two reported cases on the subject, which are more than 40 years old, probably reflect the lack of sympathy felt by courts toward the plaintiffs.

A Utah opera house complained that the dances, shows, dramas, motion picture shows, operas, and athletic events that took place in the new school building were not school-related, were unfair competition, and that school funds were being used to transport students and adults to the activities. In view of several Utah statutes, the court concluded that the board of education could authorize the activities, could allow the student body organization to operate the activities, and could provide transportation where students were actually required to participate.[12]

A Washington high school student association operated a cafeteria and candy counter in the school building not only as a service to students, but as a way to raise money to finance student activities. When challenged, the court upheld the legality of such activities.[13] In a later case, a radio station challenged the right of a school system to charge a fee to broadcast a high school football game. The court upheld the authority of the school board to charge the fee.[14]

Of more interest than legal significance was a federal district court case in 1980.[15] A regulation of the Department of Agriculture prohibiting the sale of non-nutritious foods until after lunch periods was upheld by the court. Because the sale of snack food and junk food was such a lucrative fundraising opportunity for local schools, many administrators decried the approval of these regulations.

Summary

Money and property generated from student activities belong to the school system and should be treated as such. Particular state statutes and court decisions cause generalizations about the levying of fees for activities to be impossible. If finding enough money is a principal's greatest worry, mishandling it is also the fastest way to get into trouble!

Footnotes

1. *In re* German Township Sch. Directors, 46 D. & C. 562 (Pa. D. &. C. 1942).
2. Petition of Auditors of Hatfield Township Sch. Dist., 54 A.2d 833 (Pa. Super. Ct. 1947).
3. Id. at 836.
4. Kentucky v. Collins, 379 S.W.2d 436 (Ky. App. 1964).
5. Mississippi v. Eakin, 203 So.2d 587 (Miss. 1967). *Accord* Betterson v. Stewart, 121 S.E.2d 102 (S.C. 1961).
6. Id. at 589.
7. Paulson v. Minidoka County Sch. Dist., 463 P.2d 935 (Idaho 1970).
8. Granger v. Cascade County Sch. Dist., 499 P.2d 780 (Mont. 1972).
9. Sneed v. Greensboro, 264 S.E.2d 106 (N.C. 1980).
10. Williams v. Page, 309 F. Supp. 814 (N.D. Ill. 1970).
11. Board of Educ. v. Cronin, 388 N.E.2d 72 (Ill. App. 1979).
12. Beard v. Board of Educ., 16 P.2d 900 (Utah 1932).
13. Hempel v. School Dist. No. 329, 59 P.2d 729 (Wash. 1936).
14. Colorado High Sch. Act. Ass'n. v. Uncompahgre Broadcasting Co., 300 P.2d 968 (Colo. 1956).
15. Community Nutrition Inst. v. Bergland, 493 F. Supp. 488 (D. D.C. 1980).

Appendices

Appendix A
The American Court System

Two separate court systems operate in this country—federal and state. While each system generally has jurisdiction (legal authority) in different areas of the law, in some cases, jurisdiction may overlap and choice of court systems becomes a strategic question for the lawyer to decide. Except in certain limited circumstances, cases that reach a state supreme court go no further. Figure 1 illustrates the federal judiciary court system.

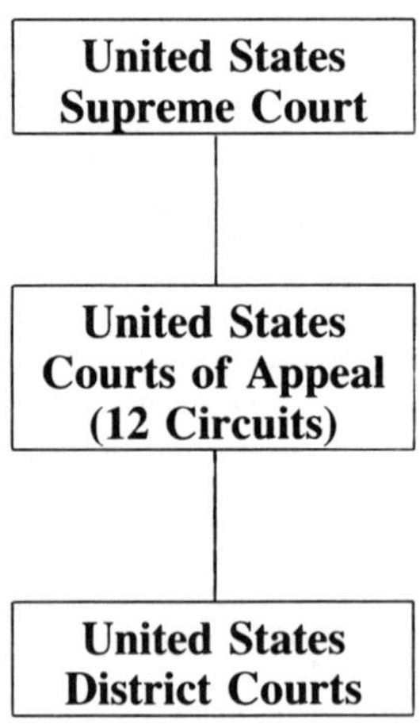

Figure 1. The Federal Judiciary

The basic federal trial court is the United States District Court, where all cases (school and otherwise) begin, where there may be a jury, and where the evidence and witnesses are presented. Each state has at least one United States District Court, although some states are further divided (e.g., United States District Court for the Northern District of Alabama, United States District Court for the Middle District of Alabama, and the United States District Court for the Southern District of Alabama.)

Several federal district judges may be assigned to hear cases for a particular district court.

A party that is unhappy with the result of the trial in the federal district court may go to the Court of Appeals for the circuit in which the federal district is located. The United States is divided geographically into 12 federal judicial circuits. The Court of Appeals for the Eleventh Circuit, for example, hears cases from federal district courts in Alabama, Georgia, and Florida.

While in some instances a right of appeal to the Supreme Court is granted by federal statutes, most cases are heard by the Supreme Court only if the Court chooses to hear the appeal. This it does in only a small percentage of cases in which review is sought—usually those cases the Court believes to have special legal or social significance.

With some exceptions, state courts operate like the federal system and most state court systems resemble the Alabama judiciary (see Figure 2).

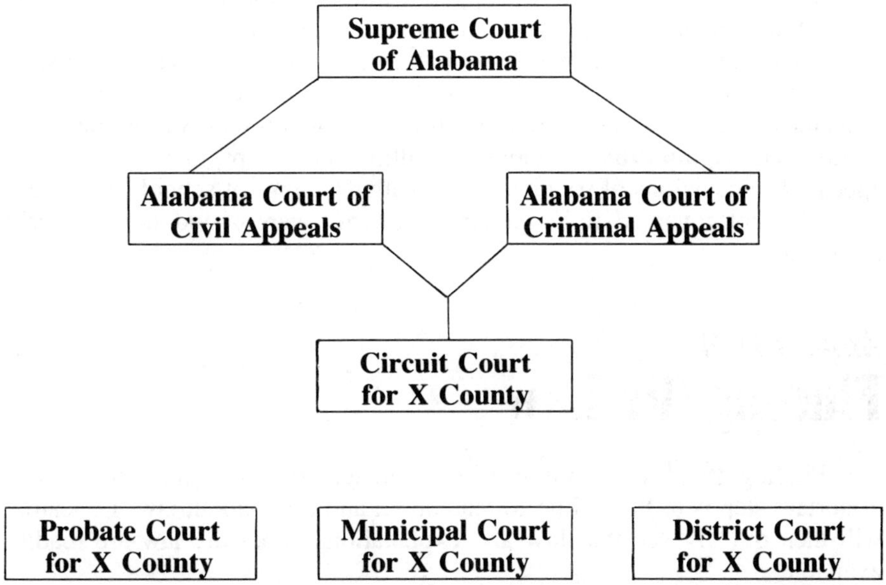

Figure 2. A Typical State Judiciary—Alabama

While Alabama has two levels of appellate courts below the state supreme court, most states have only one. Some states, like Nebraska, have no intermediate appeals court at all. State courts also have more varieties of trial courts than do federal courts. For example, while the Circuit Court for X County is the basic state trial court, other Alabama trial courts hear civil cases with lesser amounts of money involved, or criminal cases with smaller fines or shorter terms of imprisonment. Most school cases would start in a basic trial court like the Circuit Court for Mobile County, Alabama.

How does a civil (non-criminal) case get to court? The following explanation is very simplified and may not accurately reflect the exact process or terminology used for a particular state. **A knowledge of one's *own state* law is essential for intelligent legal decision making.**

The *plaintiff* starts the suit by filing a *complaint* in the court with appropriate jurisdiction. The *defendant* is the one being sued or charged. The defendant files an *answer* in response to the plaintiff's complaint. Numerous pretrial procedures, including depositions, interrogatories, and motions may follow.

Some lawsuits never make it to the trial stage; they are settled in advance by the parties or dismissed by the judge on motions of either party. In the typical civil trial, the plaintiff presents all the witnesses and evidence first and then the defendant offers rebuttal witnesses and evidence. Special rules dictate procedures to follow in commencing and conducting any lawsuit and subsequent trial.

Once a decision has been reached (with or without a jury), the losing party may exercise the right of appeal to the appropriate court. The *appellant* is the one who instigates the appeal while the *appellee,* having won the original suit, must now fight to maintain the trial court result.

On appeal, new evidence is not presented and witnesses are not heard. An appellate court is not a trial court. An appellate decision is based upon oral and written arguments from the attorneys and a review of the transcript of the trial. Again, rules establish deadlines and steps to follow for the appeal. The decisions of trial courts (as with decisions of school boards) are generally not reversed unless their judgments were found to be clearly erroneous.

Appendix B
Finding the Law

Finding the law is not nearly as difficult as educators think. The important step is to be willing to read about and think about law. Educators will then quickly see that law and explanations about the law are readily available.

For the neophyte, reading secondary sources is probably the best approach. Many excellent, up-to-date school law books are available and most professional organizations publish journals which include articles about recent legal developments. Examples of such journals are:

- *NASSP Bulletin* (National Association of Secondary School Principals)
- *National Elementary Principal* (National Association of Elementary School Principals)
- *Educational Leadership* (Association for Supervision and Curriculum Development)

Coaches' organizations and athletic and activity associations at the national and state levels also publish timely information about law.

Several profit and non-profit groups publish weekly, biweekly, and monthly newsletters that focus entirely upon law. Perhaps the best materials come from the National Organization on Legal Problems in Education (NOLPE). In addition to a monthly newsletter, NOLPE issues numerous monographs and books each year. The relatively inexpensive membership in NOLPE is an excellent investment for a principal or for a school system with limited resources.

Legal research is relatively easy. All legal citations (references) are written in the same way and all law libraries are similarly organized.

Consider the citation, 419 U.S. 565. The "419" is the volume; the "U.S." identifies the book as *United States Reports,* the official source of United States Supreme Court opinions; and the "565" is the first page of a particular opinion. Giving such a citation to any lawyer or law librarian should always produce the same result—*Goss v. Lopez,* a student rights case. Statutes and agency regulations are cited in the same fashion.

Since school law has become bigger business, two private companies have started to produce biweekly or monthly references that include only school law cases: West Publishing Company and the Bureau of National Affairs.

Where, physically, can one find statutes, regulations, and court cases? Of course, this is not a problem if a system can maintain a basic law library for itself. Most systems cannot afford such an expenditure, so other sources may be found. Check with the school system attorney. Generally, all county courthouses have a law library. State capitols usually have a public law library located near the state supreme court. All law schools have very extensive libraries. Larger law firms usually have their own libraries and may be willing to permit local educators to use the materials.

Appendix C
Reading a Case

Reading and understanding a case requires two things:

1. practice
2. some questions to answer while reading the case.

One practices reading court cases for the same reason a place kicker keeps practicing extra points: While practice may not make perfect, the reader becomes familiar with the language and concepts.

Here are eight questions that should be considered while reading a case:

- Who are the parties: plaintiff? defendant? appellant? appellee?
- What is (are) the disputed legal issue(s)?
- What are the facts or circumstances that brought about this case?
- What relief is requested of the court: money damages? injunction?
- Is this the trial court opinion or an appellate court opinion? If this is an appellate court opinion, what were the results in the lower court(s)?
- What are the plaintiff's legal arguments? defendant's legal arguments?
- Who wins here? What is the court's reasoning to support the result?
- What message(s) should the reader get from this case?

For practice, try reading one case. While practically any school case would suffice, reading *Tinker v. Des Moines Independent Community School District* would be a valuable initial experience. Any school law book that includes opinions will have *Tinker;* otherwise, go to a law library and find 393 U.S. 503 (1969).

When studying the opinion, find the answers for the eight questions previously suggested. Brief answers are included here for consideration *after* you read and analyze the *Tinker* case:

- John Tinker and other students are the plaintiffs and appellants, and the Des Moines school system and its officials are the defendants and appellees.
- Do students have First Amendment rights while at school, and when, if ever, may these rights be limited by school officials?
- After becoming aware of a planned protest of the Vietnam War, Des Moines principals adopted a rule subjecting students wearing black armbands to suspension. No evidence was offered of any disruption of schoolwork.
- Injunction and nominal damages.
- Appellate court. The trial court dismissed the complaint after evidence was presented. The Court of Appeals for the Eighth Circuit, all judges sitting *(en banc),* divided equally, thus upholding the trial court decision.
- Students can exercise free speech in the school setting under non-disrupting circumstances v. vast discretion of school authorities to control student conduct.
- Plaintiff (Tinker). Students and teachers have First Amendment rights even while at school. The burden is on the school to justify any limitations by presenting evidence of material and substantial disruption of the school environment.
- Students and teachers have rights while at school, when properly exercised.